The Bookie's Runner

Brendan Gisby

Copyright © 2010 Brendan Gisby
All rights reserved.
ISBN: 1482038927
ISBN-13: 978-1482038927

A McStorytellers publication

http://www.mcstorytellers.com

In memory of Derry McKay.

Contents

Foreword   6

Chapter One: *A Big Emptiness*   7

Chapter Two: *The Unwanted Son*   10

Chapter Three: *Round the World*   15

Chapter Four: *A Fairy-Tale Marriage*   19

Chapter Five: *So Many Children*   24

Chapter Six: *The Good Times*   27

Chapter Seven: *A Pair of Scavengers*   31

Chapter Eight: *The Black Sheep*   35

Chapter Nine: *The Big Garden*   43

Chapter Ten: *A Runner for the Bookie*   60

Chapter Eleven: *The Bad Times*   63

Chapter Twelve: *The Aga Khan*   67

Chapter Thirteen: *A Reward in Heaven*   87

About the Author   89

"He's dressed like Frank Sinatra, like a member of the Rat Pack. He's the bookie's runner with the lopsided grin, but he's destined to lose."

Foreword

Many people have written books about their fathers. In doing so, they have set out to celebrate their fathers' heroism or achievements or fame – or even notoriety. I've written this short book about my father. He wasn't a hero. Apart from fathering seven children, six of whom are alive and kicking to this day, he didn't achieve anything noteworthy in his brief life. He wasn't famous in any way. Nor was he remotely notorious. On the contrary, he was respected and loved by all who knew him. He was an ordinary, working-class man; a gentle soul, who loved his family and toiled day and night for them.

So why did I want to write a book about him? The answer is simple. Dad was also a downtrodden man; one of life's losers. His experiences – the events that came together to destroy him – are important to me. They shaped my outlook on life. They made me who I am.

Brendan Gisby
August 2010

Chapter One
A Big Emptiness

The bus is climbing up Kirkliston Road now on its way out of the town. It has just gone past the end of our street. In a moment, it will pass the entrance to the cemetery, where Dad is buried alongside little Patricia and old Dan. In about an hour's time, it will pull up in front of St Mary's Academy in Bathgate. And so will begin the first day of a new school year and my first day in the Fourth Year.

I'm glad that I managed to get a seat on my own at the back of the bus. I can sit here quietly, staring out of the window, watching the fields roll by, the greyness of the sky above them matching how I feel this morning. I'm also relieved that no-one spoke to me at the bus stop. Just one word from any of them or the flicker of a smile or catching their eyes for only a second would have been enough to break my resolve and have me bursting into tears like a sissy. But they all knew that it was best to stay away from me, thank God.

It won't be the same when I get to St Mary's. None of my pals will know that my Dad died during the school holidays. I won't be telling them either. I'm just going to have to smile and laugh and joke along with them and get through this awful day without breaking down. Right now, I'm on the verge of crying. There's a lump in my throat and a knot in my stomach. There's a terrible feeling of dread hanging over me; it's like a big emptiness. I miss my Dad so much. It feels like this is the worst and loneliest day of my life.

Memories of Dad, glimpses of him, are crowding into my thoughts. Some are good memories, but most are sad. They're not in any particular order either; some are from years ago, while others are much more recent. And they're all jostling for place.

Here's one of him standing at the bus stop that I've just come from. He's holding that little suitcase of his, waiting serenely for the bus that will take him into the hospital, convinced that he's only going in for tests and that he'll be back in a few days.

'Look after your mother, now,' he's saying to me, but I can't hear the words.

Here's one of him a few days later. He's lying on his hospital bed. It's the day after he won his big bet and had the first operation. There's a wry, pained grin on his face.

And here's a happier one of him when I was a lot younger. He's splashing about in the sea, wearing a pair of Mum's blue knickers and claiming to have swum out to Inchgarvie and back.

He's almost skipping along the street in the next one. There's a thick, woollen scarf wrapped around his mouth. That was the time when my sister, Mary, 'found' the money that he needed for the dentist.

He's happy and cheerful in the next one, too, pouring tea for me and my pals from school on the day the road bridge was opened.

But here's another sad one. It's just after Patricia's funeral. Dad is sliding with his back down the living room door. Now he's sitting on the floor, erupting in big, hot tears. We were all little then. We're crying, too, and smothering him in hugs, trying to console him.

And here's a more recent one of him sitting with his head in his hands at the kitchen table. There's a frightened, hunted look in his eyes. He's just discovered that the vanity case has been broken into again and emptied of the weekend's returns. The bitch had found his new hiding place for it. The fucking bitch! Why did she have to do that to him?

I have to stop this. There are tears misting my eyes. I can hardly see out of the window now. That's the War memorial in Kirkliston out there, I think; it looks like a grey blur. I need to concentrate. I need to control the anger and bitterness that are welling up inside of me, or they'll overwhelm me and I won't last this journey. If I can use the time that's left here in the quiet of the bus to put the jumble of memories into some sort of order, perhaps I'll be able to figure out who my Dad was, where he came from and what he did in life. And perhaps then I'll be able to understand why he had to suffer and why he died like he did.

Chapter Two

The Unwanted Son

It's funny, but now that I come to think about it, I don't really know very much about Dad when he was younger. He never seemed to talk about his past life. What little I do know I've learned from Mum, and she has a habit of getting things mixed up and sometimes exaggerating or twisting them. What I am certain of is that Dad was born in England. That made him English, I suppose. I've never thought about him that way before, but being English and not Scottish didn't make him any less of a person in my eyes. He was christened with two very English names – Charles Frederick. You'd think that he would have been called Charlie or Chick or even Derrick, but for some reason he ended up being called Derry. I've never heard of anyone else with that name.

As far as I can remember, I've never met Dad's father, my grandfather. I don't even know if the man is still alive; he wasn't at Dad's funeral, that's for sure. I know that he's called Tom and that he lives in Kent – or at least he did. He used to be a sailor, I think. Mum says that he came from a long line of seafarers, who hailed originally from Norway, although she might have made that up. According to her, there's quite a mixture of blood running in our veins. There's Irish from her side, along with a bit of Spanish, or so she claims. And there's Scottish, English and Norwegian from Dad's side. And Jewish, of course; mustn't forget that. She said once that there was some Jewish blood in Tom's family, on his mother's side, which accounted for Dad's swarthy looks and that hooked nose of his. She also said that if Hitler had managed to invade Britain, Dad would have been done for. I'm sort of sceptical about that as well. I *think* that Dad was circumcised, though. So maybe the last bit was true. It's difficult to tell with Mum and her romantic notions.

Anyway, Tom and Dad's Mum, Annie, our Nana, got divorced when Dad was still a little boy. Tom got married again and had other children. I've seen a picture of his second wife with Dad's stepsister and two stepbrothers, but I've never met any of them.

Nana left Kent and came back to the Ferry with Dad. She also remarried and had other children – my Uncle John and my Aunt Cathie – by Cherry, my granddad. I'm not sure whether it was because Cherry and her were overcrowded in their place or because Annie couldn't cope with Dad and two younger children, but Dad went to live with Annie's mother and father, his grandparents, Dan and Kate McKay. They all stayed in the Crossroads, just along the road from each other.

Dan died when I was a baby, but old Kate's still going strong, living on her own in the same house, as tough and independent as ever. She's our great-grandmother, but we call her Gran, just like Dad did. She must be well into her eighties now, yet she's still tramping up and down the braes, doing her paper-round, and smoking her Woodbines and drinking her gill of whisky a day.

Mum says that Kate and Dan fought all the time, and that Dan was a mean, old bugger, who used to batter Kate and kick her cat when he was drunk. He was a soldier in the First World War, but the war apparently turned him sour. There's a framed picture of him in his soldier's uniform hanging in Nana's living room. When you pass the picture, he glowers down at you with that proud look of his and those fierce whiskers. He's sitting in his bonnet and kilt, a big sword hanging at his side. Gran's still got that sword in her house. It's black and blunt now, but she uses it to chop the kindling.

As well as Annie, Kate and Dan had a son called Jock, who was killed in Normandy in the Second World War. Jock was posthumously awarded the Military Medal, for courage on the field of action. His name is inscribed on the memorial plaque that's on the wall below the Jubilee clock in the High Street. I wonder if Dad was there the day that Kate and Dan received the news about Jock. Their house must have been an awful sad place that day.

Kate's quite a legend in the Ferry, really. I remember she came to visit us one afternoon a few years ago. She sat talking to Mum in the living room for hours, with us kids listening in, fascinated by her stories.

'It's been a long life, right enough, Mary,' she said at one point. 'Some of it good. A hellish lot of it bad. It's the wildness in me that's kept me going. The good times are the ones to remember. I could spend all day talking about them and still not be finished. The weddings. The funerals; aye, sometimes. The christenings. Diddling my bairns on my knee, and my grandbairns, and my great grandbairns. The Hogmanay parties: fu' to the gunnels, singing like a lintie, jigging like auld Nick, the De'il himself. The Ferry Fairs. Christ, I shinnied up the Greasy Pole every year until I was near to sixty!'

Stopping to light another Woodbine, she stared into the clouds of smoke and clucked quietly.

'Aye, the good times. Gone now, though, and all my friends with them. Even auld Johnnie's dead. Christ, I knew him for years, Mary, since we were bairns. My, what times we had, what parties, with Johnnie and his auld fiddle!

'And who can forget the Ferry Fairs when Killiecrankie turned up, fu' as a puggy, with the red Heilan' jacket and the sodjer's bunnet and the pair of black boots tied to the pike over his shoulder. What a sight he was! He would ring the toon crier's bell, the one he kept polished all year, and he would belt out the proclamation at the top of his voice. Aye, Killiecrankie and me, we'd drink and sing and dance the night away…'

Poor Gran. She was too upset to come to Dad's funeral. Mum said it was because she was scared to go to the cemetery and see Dan's grave again, knowing that she would be lying beside him in a few years' time. She once told Mum that she could feel that wicked old man chuckling with glee, biding his time, waiting for Kate to join him.

'He was bad to me in life, Mary,' she had said. 'What'll he be like in eternity?'

Well, that might not have been her only reason for staying away from the funeral. I heard some people say she couldn't bear the pain of knowing that she had outlived her grandson, the little boy whom she had raised and was so close to. Because that's right: as far as people in the Ferry were concerned back then, Dad was brought up by Kate and Dan as if he was their own son. He even took their name, being known to everyone to this day as Derry McKay.

Imagine how that would feel if it happened to you. You're a little boy. You're taken away from your father, who's no longer interested in you, and your mother farms you out to your granny. Both your mother and father are now more intent on raising their new families. You're treated as the unwanted son. Then you lose your own name and become someone else, like an orphan. I would've been hurt and lonely and devastated by it all, but none of it seemed to have affected Dad. Right up until about a year ago, he was forever cheerful and happy-go-lucky. In spite of the problems and the lack of money, he always acted as if he was riding on the crest of a wave. Once, years ago, I remember walking with him down to the High Street. For the whole of that journey, he had a smile and a nice word for every single person we passed, and they for him. Even though he was brought up by Kate and Dan, and he had that wild, Highland McKay blood in him, he didn't possess any of their fierceness. He was the opposite of them: softer and more refined. There was a gentleness in him that he must have inherited from his father.

    Fuck! Thinking about Dad like that is making me want to bubble again. I'll be snivelling soon if I'm not careful. I need to close my eyes tight, to concentrate, to think about the next part of his story.

Chapter Three
Round the World

That's the thing, though: apart from him living in the Crossroads and being brought up by Kate and Dan, I don't know anything at all about Dad when he was growing up. I suppose that he went to the Protestant school at the top of Distillery Brae – it was the only school in the town at the time – but I've no idea who his pals were or where he played or what he did as a boy. The next thing I do know is that he joined the Royal Navy as soon as he was old enough. There's a picture of him back in the house. He's wearing his sailor's uniform in it and he's got a big grin on his face. He doesn't look much older than I am now.

By the time Dad joined up, the War was just ending, so he didn't see any action, or at least that's what he told us. I wonder how he felt about that. If it was me, I think I would have been relieved. I think enough people had been killed by that time. He served on the aircraft carrier, HMS Victorious, as an Ordinary Seaman. I know that for sure because I read his discharge papers. They're in that box that Mum keeps the important papers in – birth certificates and such like.

Dad talked quite a lot about his time in the Navy. I think he was grateful for the chance that it gave him to go round the world.

Although his ship wasn't involved in any action, he said it waited off the coast of Japan after the bomb was dropped on Hiroshima. Then it sailed into Tokyo, where he was befriended by a Japanese family. He stayed with them on their houseboat for a while. I remember him remarking on more than one occasion that, despite all the devastation and poverty around them, they were very clean people. He brought a beautiful kimono back with him from Japan, but the thing is totally ruined now after years of us kids dressing up in it.

There's that story he used to tell about being on Shore Patrol – it was in Hong Kong Harbour, I think – when the Chinese began to riot. He and another member of the Patrol heard a mob of rioters heading in their direction, so they quickly took off their white armbands and belts, threw them and their batons into the harbour, and walked away in the opposite direction. Mum says that that wasn't a cowardly thing to do; it was just smart, and it probably saved their lives. I really like that story.

There's also the one about him serving soup from a big urn on deck when the ship was at sea one day. While the ratings were queuing up to get their soup, a Petty Officer, who had been bullying Dad for weeks, kept nipping at him until Dad finally snapped, picked up the urn and poured its contents over the man. Luckily for both of them, the soup was lukewarm. Dad was put on jankers for that, but I don't think there was any more bullying afterwards. I like that story as well. It shows that Dad wasn't all meekness and gentleness. Maybe he did have some of that McKay fierceness in him after all.

And there's the amazing thing that happened to Dad when his ship was in Perth, Australia. He met an older sailor, an Australian, in a bar. The man asked him where about in Scotland he came from.

'Edinburgh,' Dad replied, presuming that the man would never have heard of Queensferry.

'Hell, mate,' said the man, 'I was based not far from Edinburgh for a spell during the War. At the Port Edgar naval base. There's a little village just next to the base by the name of Queensferry. A real friendly place. I met this wonderful, old lady there. She made us all welcome. The life and soul of the party, mate. She was called Kate... Kate McKay. A wonderful lady.'

Incredible! Dad went to the other side of the world to meet someone by chance who praised his own granny, the woman who brought him up. Kate's a legend in her own lifetime, all right.

Now, what else happened to Dad when he was in the Navy? Oh, yes, he learned to swim. He said that his crewmates threw him overboard one day, and that it was a case of him either swimming or drowning. I only saw him swimming the once, and from what I remember he was pretty good at it. It was that day when we all went down to the shore for a picnic. I don't know what age I was, but I must have been pretty young, because I still thought that France was on the other side of the water. Anyway, after we had eaten, Dad suddenly stripped off his shirt and vest and trousers and stood there in a pair of light blue knickers, which he must have taken from Mum's drawer and put on in the house.

'Right,' he said, 'I'm off for a swim.'

'You eejit, Derry,' Mum laughed. 'You'll get arrested if anyone catches you in those.'

'Nobody'll see me when I'm in the water, hen,' he shrugged.

He told me that he was going to swim out to Inchgarvie, the island out there in the middle of the Forth, the one beside the Forth

Bridge. It seemed a long way away to me.

'Don't be stupid,' Mum shouted to him, but he rushed down the shore and into the water.

I watched him swim away until his head was just a speck and then disappeared altogether. When he came back, he said that he had been on the island. I remember being impressed by that back then, but I'm sure now that he was only kidding me.

The only other thing that I can think of about Dad being in the Navy was the habit that he picked up of frying everything he cooked. The doctors in the Ferry made a big thing of that. They told him that he should lay off fried food, because it was contributing to his ulcer. He couldn't, of course. They never said anything about the constant worry and the backbreaking work. Mum is bitter about those doctors. She says that she's going to sue them for their incompetence. She won't, of course. I think that she's just using words to cover up her own guilt...

Chapter Four

A Fairy-Tale Marriage

I can see that we're in Winchburgh now. We've just turned off Main Street at the Tally-Ho Inn. There, away in the distance, is the first of the big red shale bings that dominate the landscape between here and Broxburn. The Union Canal is on my right. And here on my left the bus is passing the Holy Family, the little primary school that I used to go to until they built the new one in the Ferry. I can remember the first day that I went to the Holy Family. It was ... Actually, it must have been ten years ago to this day. I was only five. Dad came with me on the bus. It wasn't a school bus like today – there weren't any for us Catholic kids back then – but the usual scheduled one for Broxburn. It was a double-decker. We were on the bottom deck, and I was at the window on the left-hand side of the bus, just like now. I was sitting on a newspaper that Dad had put down to help reduce the vibrations and stop me being ...

 God, it's just not fucking fair! Everything that I look at this morning is reminding me of Dad and making me want to cry. People will begin to stare at me in a moment. I'm going to have to dry my eyes and concentrate again and pick up the story from the time when Dad came back from the Navy. That's where Mum comes into it, I suppose. And Mum has quite a story of her own. In fact, I probably know more about her when she was younger than I do about Dad.

I know that she came over from Eire during the War to work in service for Lord Rosebery in Mentmore Towers in Somerset. 'Another fresh, young Irish girl, straight off the farm' is how she describes it. She's got a picture of herself standing at the foot of the steps going up to Mentmore Towers. With those giant stone urns on either side of her, she looks so small and waiflike in the picture. She told us that, coming from a neutral country, she was classified as an alien for the duration of the War. She also said that when she first came over she was really only a simple, country girl and very naïve as a result, especially about things like swearing. There's the story that she often tells about the winter's morning when she and the rest of the staff were having breakfast at the big table in the servants' quarters. Everyone was very polite and talking about the weather. Wanting to join in on the conversation, Mum announced to the assembled company that it was 'cold enough to freeze the balls off a brass monkey'. She had heard someone say that the day before, but she had no idea what it meant. Needless to say, the whole table had fallen about laughing.

Because Mum was employed as an upstairs maid, she had to travel along with the rest of the staff whenever Lord Rosebery came up to Dalmeny House, his stately home in Scotland, which is just along the road from the Ferry. According to many people, Rosebery owns not only Dalmeny House and the estate that it's on, but also the very land that the Ferry is built on. Even our own street is named after him.

Mum used to tell us stories about her time in service. She said that Rosebery was an old skinflint. Even though he had enough money to buy a brand new pair of pyjamas for every night of the rest of his life, her job each evening before his lordship retired was to darn the tears in the one pair of pyjamas that he always wore. She also told us about Rosebery's son, Neil – she calls him 'young Lord Primrose' – and the times at Dalmeny House when he and his friends drank champagne into the early hours of the morning and cavorted naked in the courtyard fountain.

'That was during the years of so-called austerity after the War, of course,' she complained, 'when there was rationing for the likes of us and champagne for the toffs.'

After Mum left Dalmeny House to settle in the Ferry, Lord Rosebery's butler, Chaddie, and his housekeeper, Grace, who were married to each other, used to come to visit her – 'young Mary', they continued to call her – and her new family every time they travelled up from Mentmore Towers. They're nice people, Chaddie and Grace, but I haven't seen them for a long time now.

I think that Mum is as Irish as you could ever get. She says that she was born and brought up on a farm in County Cavan, close to the border with Ulster, in Rebel country. She loves Michael Collins with a passion, and she hates Eamon De Valéra with a vengeance. 'Slimy toad' she spits out whenever the latter man's name is mentioned in the papers or on the radio or television. She claims that her father was a Lieutenant-Colonel in the Irish Republican Army, one of Michael Collins' right-hand men. Like most people, I used to be sceptical about that claim. But about a year ago she showed me a book that she had just bought. It's in the bookcase now back at home. It's a biography of Michael Collins, a paperback. On the front cover there's a picture of 'The Big Fella' in his uniform, with the Irish tricolour in the background. And in the

Index at the back there's an entry about my grandfather – 'Lane, Padraig, Lt.-Col., IRA' it reads. I became a believer after seeing that. It was because of it that I began to develop a big interest in Irish history, especially about the Easter Rising in 1916.

Apart from De Valéra, Mum also hates the British Army – 'the English Army' she calls it – for all the injustices that it committed in her home country over many years. She has a special contempt for Winston Churchill. She can never forgive his creation, the Black and Tans, for what they did to her father after they captured him. They ripped out his fingernails, wrapped a Union Jack around him and paraded him that way through his own village. According to Mum, the shame haunted the poor man for the rest of his life, so much so that he eventually took to drink, neglecting his farm and family; her mother fell ill and was taken to a sanatorium; and she and her sister and brothers were put in a home that was run by nuns. When she heard a few months ago that Churchill was close to dying, she laughed and said she would dance a jig on his grave. She's not a forgiving Irishwoman.

When I think about all of that, I suppose that Mum had a much harder time than Dad when she was growing up: losing her father to drink and her mother to illness; being left alone to look after her sister and brothers; and then being separated from them when she and they were taken away and put in different homes. At least Dad did have his granny to look after him and his mother just along the road.

Anyway, Mum used to come up to Dalmeny House with Lord Rosebery. That's obviously how she got to know the Ferry and to meet Dad. I'm not sure how they met, but I think it was at a dance in the Town Hall. Mum says that Dad was a great dancer. I can picture him now, probably still in his Navy uniform, stepping lightly across the dance floor, his arm around Mum's waist, just like Fred Astaire. Yes, there they both are: the handsome, charming, gentle, young man from the Ferry and the pretty colleen with the soft lilt, blue-black hair and hazel eyes. It's a match made in heaven. Theirs will be a fairy-tale marriage. They'll produce beautiful children and live happily ever after. Aye, if only...

Chapter Five

So Many Children

So Mum and Dad got married. The wedding was in the Ferry. There's a photo of it in the house somewhere, with the happy couple posing in front of the Chapel and the wedding guests standing on either side of them. From the number of guests, it looks like it was a pretty big affair. All the family guests would have come from Dad's side, of course, with no-one there from Ireland to represent Mum.

After they were married, they stayed with Nana for a while and then someplace in Edinburgh. Or it might have been the other way round. Whatever way it was, they ended up in the Ferry, living in a tenement in Clark Place. That building was demolished years ago. It stood right next to where the Villas are, backing on to the distillery's railway yard. Mum says it was a slum property that was full of rats, which you could hear gnawing through the walls at night. I don't know about that, but my earliest memory comes from there. I think I was only two or three years old. We must have stayed quite low down in the building – in the basement, maybe – because I can remember looking up from my cot through a barred window to see old Maude's wheels clanking past. Maude was the steam engine that up until quite recently carried grain from Edinburgh to the distillery. She was built before the turn of the century and saw service in France during the First World War. Everyone used to refer to her as an old lady, but she was actually named after a man, Lieutenant-General Maude of the Coldstream Guards, who captured Baghdad from the Turks in 1917.

It couldn't have been long after then that we were allocated one of the houses that were being built for the Council up at the back of the town, because my next earliest memory is of all of us visiting the building site to see how they were getting on with our new house. I think Gran was there as well that day. I remember copying one of the workers by spitting into a lavatory pan that was lying outside the house and waiting to be installed. Mum gave me a row for that.

Anyway, the house that we were allocated was a semi-detached one with front, back and side gardens; a kitchen, living room and bathroom downstairs; and three bedrooms upstairs. Mum and Dad must have thought that it was a million miles different from Clark Place. By the time we moved into it, they would have had four children already – Ann Marie, the first-born, then me, then Lena, then Mary, with only about a year separating each of us. Then Patricia came along. She was actually born in the new house, in the big bedroom; the only one of us not born in a hospital, I think. She died of measles when she was still a toddler. I'll never forget that sight of Dad sliding down the living room door and dissolving into tears when he came back from her funeral. He must have held the tears in all through the funeral and right up until he saw us. We were waiting in the room, being looked after by a neighbour. We were all so young then, but instinctively we crowded round him and tried to cuddle away his tears...

God, that's me starting to cry again. Shut your eyes tight.

Get that image out of your head. Think of what happens next with the family. Oh, yes, there was a gap of a few years and then Bernadette was born. I can remember there being quite a to-do about her name. Dad wanted to call her Roslyn for some reason, but Mum insisted that the name should be Bernadette, another good old Irish one. Much to Mum's annoyance, Dad went ahead and registered the birth in the name of Roslyn. Although we all call her that at home, Mum has made sure that she's known as Bernadette everywhere else, especially at school. The wee lassie has two names now. It's all very confusing.

After Bernadette, there was another gap of a few years before Shaun appeared. He's the bairn of the family. He'll be five soon and starting primary school this morning. Needless to say, there's never been any confusion about his name; it couldn't be more Irish.

That's the family, then: Mum and Dad and the six of us, the brood. Some people say that Catholics breed like rabbits because of the Pope's ban on contraception, but I'm sure that wasn't the case with Mum and Dad. I think they just wanted to have a big family. There weren't any additions to it after Shaun, though. The doctors warned Mum that her heart would give out if she got pregnant again. And that's just as well, I suppose, because she was already like the woman in that nursery rhyme. You know the one. The old woman who lived in a shoe. She had so many children she didn't know what to do.

Chapter Six
The Good Times

We're surrounded by giant pink shale bings now. The bus seems tiny as it winds its way through them. I've seen this sight every school day for the last three years, but it never fails to fascinate me. I always imagine that we're really in cowboy country. The Bad Lands. Apache territory. Our stagecoach is thundering through a dry gulch. It has just escaped an ambush. Soon it will be rolling into the rough frontier town of Broxburn…

But I don't want to pretend like that this morning. I want to think about that big family of ours instead. We were poor when we were all little, that was for sure, but we always managed to get by. And we were happy, too. At least, that's how I recall it. Those were the good times, I suppose.

Dad appeared to be around much more back then. During the week, he would come home from his job in the dockyard, strip to the waist, and wash and shave at the kitchen sink, all the time singing at the top of his voice.

Sometimes in the summer after tea, we would all go out for a walk up through the little woods at the end of our street, along Lovers' Lane to Dalmeny village and then back. I remember one time when we were in Lovers' Lane when Dad suddenly reached into a bush and then quickly pulled back his arm to show us some pale-blue, speckled eggs in the palm of his hand.

'A blackbird's nest,' he whispered excitedly before carefully replacing the eggs.

Not forgetting Friday evenings, of course, when the four oldest of us would wait for Dad outside the dockyard gates. As soon as the hooter went and the gates were opened, he'd appear among the crowd of men, wheeling his bike, grinning when he saw us. Then he'd take us along the High Street to McGillivary's little sweetshop, where he'd open up his pay packet and hand each of us the money to buy a lucky bag, our weekly treat.

And sometimes at weekends, we would go on picnics, like that one on the shore when Dad wore Mum's knickers, or we would take trips on the ferryboat over to Dunfermline Glen for the day. There was that time when we were all leaving the ferryboat in North Queensferry to catch the bus for Dunfermline, and Mum warned me about walking too close to the edge of the pier.

'If you fall in and drown, I'll kill you,' she shouted in her special Irish way.

God, she's always saying daft things like that, talking about television 'serious' instead of 'series' and people going through 'phrases' instead of 'phases' and the 'cat' fitting instead of the 'cap'. Once, she called the poster of Scotland in my bedroom a 'giraffical' map. Sometimes it's funny, but other times it's just embarrassing, especially when it's said in front of my pals. It was funny that time in North Queensferry, though. Dad laughed out loud. Then the rest of us joined in, even Mum.

We older kids seemed to enjoy ourselves a lot more, too. I can just picture the four of us leaving the house along with the two boys from next door. It's a beautiful August morning, with hardly a cloud in the sky. It looks like it's going to be another hot day. We're on our way down to the sea, to spend the day at the Shellbeds.

We're like a swarm as we head along the street; all six of us buzzing and moving in a noisy, excited cluster. We swarm around the corner, where the Caseys live with their ferocious dog. The dog looks like Black Bob from 'The Dandy', but it's demented and out of control. It usually prowls around the Caseys' front garden, growling and snarling and snapping at passers-by from behind the fence. Sometimes the Caseys leave the garden gate open, deliberately, just to be cruel, and the dog will patrol the pavement instead, scaring people, defying them to get past. If any one of us children are on our own, or even if there are two or three of us, we'll make a wide detour to avoid the Caseys. But not today. Today we are invincible.

Sure enough, the dog is there when we pass, barking wildly as soon as it sees us. One of us – my sister, Mary, probably – decides to antagonise it by kicking the fence. The dog goes apoplectic, barking more loudly, slavering, jumping at the fence, threatening to get over. Laughing and whooping, we all run like the wind to the bottom of the hill, where we stop to get our breath back before swarming along Station Road in the direction of Dalmeny railway station and then on to the Shellbeds for more adventures...

The point is that we were all happy then. And Dad was happy, too; always laughing and singing and joking, like he loved his life and his big family. Christ, it was only a year ago that he was acting daft in front of some of my school pals. Four of them had cycled to the Ferry to watch the Queen opening the road bridge. Two had come all the way from Bathgate itself. Mum had gone off on a family visit to Ireland, her first since she had left the country, and she had taken Ann Marie with her. Dad was left to look after the rest of the kids. In the afternoon, he made my pals something to eat before they cycled back. I can see him now, standing at the kitchen table and holding the teapot up high so that it's pouring in a long dribble.

'High tea, anyone,' he's saying in a fake, posh voice …

So how come that less than a year later he's lying on a hospital bed with stitches across his belly and looking like something out of Belsen concentration camp? Where did it go wrong? Well, I know the answer. I've never said it to anyone before – not even to myself – but, as far as I'm concerned, Mum was to blame for it all. It was her who was obsessed with making sure that we were always turned out well. It was her who kept telling us that, despite our lack of money, we were a cut above everyone else. She even claimed once that we were descended from the Kings of Ireland; that we had royal blood in us, for fuck's sake! Sure, Mum, we had an immaculate house and proper school uniforms and nice clothes to wear to the Chapel on Sunday. But didn't you realise that we couldn't afford those things? Didn't it occur to you that we didn't really *need* them? Didn't it dawn on you that the clothes and the furniture and the carpets were all bought on tick and would have to be paid for one day?

Sometimes I think that Mum was just stupid, acting like that simple farm girl. But that doesn't make what she did right. The plain fact of the matter is that, while Dad was away out every day knocking his pan in, she was piling up the debt and making promises to more and more tallymen.

Chapter Seven

A Pair of Scavengers

There's an ornament that I once saw on someone's mantelpiece. It was a little statue of Andy Capp with a big grin on his face and both his trouser pockets turned inside out. At his feet, there was a caption which read 'Rent Spent'. I've always thought that that ornament kind of summed up our family. When we were younger, we were happy enough, but we were also forever hard up, just like Andy Capp. None of us kids were ever given pocket money. And none of us went on school trips like the other kids. There was never enough money for any of those things. Before the end of every week, Mum and Dad were always scraping the pennies together, trying to make things last until pay day. That's what happens, I suppose, when you have too many mouths to feed and not enough money coming in.

  I remember once when I was just a little boy going with Dad down to the shore at the Hawes Pier. It was very early on a Sunday morning, the tide was out and no-one was about. We must have been particularly hard up at that time, because we were there to search for Forth Bridge money. If you don't know what that is, it's coins – pennies usually, but also threepenny bits and sixpences, even florins and half-crowns on occasion – which have been tossed into the Forth for good luck by train passengers crossing the bridge and which are then washed ashore by the tide. You can recognise Forth Bridge money from its blue-green colour – verdigris, I think it's called. Plenty of it circulates in the Ferry, always collected secretly like that morning and stained in the same way.

    I can picture the scene as if it's happening right now in front of my eyes. It's overcast, just like this morning. I can see the shore: it's an expanse of black mud and wet, slimy rocks and glistening seaweed that slopes down to the far end of the pier. Seaweed also clings to and envelops the exposed feet of the granite pillars that straddle the shore. It will be some time yet before the waves return to surround the pillars and the water is high enough for the first ferryboat service of the day to commence. With no traffic on the road above and the town still asleep, there are no sounds, only the distant cries of the handful of gulls wheeling in the wide grey sky high above the estuary. Soon, though, the silence will be shattered when the first northbound train thunders its way across the bridge.

    Two figures, a man and a small boy, both clad in black, are picking their way through the mud, their backs stooped, their heads bent low, like a pair of scavengers. The man is wearing a red kerchief round his neck and carrying a small sack. The man is Dad, of course, and the boy is me. I think I'm only eight years old, which means that Dad is barely in his thirties.

    You can tell that I haven't done this before. Standing a few feet to the side of Dad and slightly behind him, I watch him carefully and then try to copy his actions; looking underneath the rocks, lifting the fronds of seaweed and shaking them, scouring the mud for the tiniest glints of copper or brass or silver. Suddenly, there's a big grin on my face. I've spotted the flash of a florin. It's there among those moss-covered boulders, at the bottom of a little pool of water left by the departing tide. Wait, though. In my haste to reach down for the coin, I slip on the wet moss and fall forward, my hands outstretched instinctively to lessen the impact of the fall. Dad is beside me in moments, helping me up, consoling me, examining the palm of my left hand. One of the lines across the palm has opened up and is seeping blood. I'm crying now. Speaking softly to me, Dad takes off his kerchief and ties it tightly round my hand. After a short while, my tears subside. I say that I'm fine now, so we continue with our search for a while longer. Dad is not convinced, though. He watches me for some moments. I have remained in the same spot since the fall, probably not daring to move again. My clothes are wet and muddy. Dad is sure that I'm shivering. It's time to go, he decides. There's a fair weight in the sack already. It's been a good morning's work, a good haul.

Soon we'll begin the trek back home. The slow climb up the steps of Jacob's Ladder. The long trudge along the path that runs parallel with the railway line. Then along Station Road and up the hill to our own street. Feeling awkward in our muddy clothes, we'll nod sheepishly to people we pass in the street; neighbours, dressed in their Sunday best, on their way to chapel. Once we are home, Dad will soak the coins in a basin of soapy water. Later, he'll scrub the coins with a nailbrush. He'll clean off the mud and the slime, but he won't be able to remove the telltale blue-green signs. When he has finished cleaning the coins, Dad will be chided again by Mum. She has already scolded him for bringing me back soiled and hurt, and for showing up the family by what she calls 'parading our poverty in front of the neighbours'. Now she'll complain about the money, as if it carries a stigma.

'You can scrub it all you like, Derry,' she'll say sharply, her brogue accentuated by her annoyance, 'but it'll always look and smell of the Forth Bridge.'

Dad will smile and shrug. 'I'm just trying to help,' he'll reply. Then he'll add, 'There's no shame in being poor, Mary'.

I'm looking at the shore again. The little boy has gone, but Dad is still there. He's still wearing the red kerchief round his neck and the sack over his shoulder, but he's like a ghost now. He's waving to me and smiling that lopsided smile of his. He's saying something, but I can't make out the words.

'Have a good life, son,' I think he's mouthing.

'I'm sorry, Dad. Sorry for falling and cutting my hand,' I want to shout, but the ghost is fading way…

Chapter Eight
The Black Sheep

Fuck! That's me wanting to bubble again. I need to get that vision of Dad as a ghost out of mind, to think of something more pleasant, something with a happier ending. What about the time when the black sheep turned into an angel?

I remember that day very clearly as well. I must have been ten or eleven at the time. I was out at the front of the house, swinging on our garden gate. The gate is square and made of cast iron and painted black, and it was just the right size for me to swing on. By standing on the bottom rail, pushing my knees through the bars and resting my elbows on the top rail, I could make the gate swing back and forward, back and forward, only occasionally being required to put one foot on the ground and push the gate in order to refresh its momentum. But I needed to be gentle, otherwise the gate would clang shut and I would have to start all over again.

I would go out there to swing on the gate whenever I wanted some peace from the hubbub going on back in the house or if I needed to think about something or simply if I had nothing else to do. I liked the tranquillity that the movement gave me. Feeling safe behind the gate, I also liked to watch events on the street: people passing by or tending their gardens or going to and from the succession of vendors' vans.

Sometimes I would think I was a younger (and much quieter) version of Jimmy Martin, the man who used to live a few doors along from us. Jimmy often sat for hours on end at the open window of his front room. He also watched the comings and goings on the street, but where he and I differed was his habit of shouting out insults at the people he saw, his big, rough voice reverberating off the houses. Although some of the older women became alarmed when Jimmy shouted and wouldn't venture out on the street if he was sitting there, most people regarded him as a bit of a nuisance, a harmless crank.

Mum used to say that one day the men in white coats would come and cart Jimmy off to the loony bin, but that was before she invited him into her kitchen for a cup of tea – she always does that with waifs and strays – and learned his story. It seemed that Jimmy had been captured by the Germans early on in the War. He spent the remainder of the War working down a salt mine in France. He and his fellow prisoners weren't treated badly, though, and they got on quite well with their guards. One day, when the Germans realised that the War was lost, the guards took Jimmy and the other prisoners down the mine and told them that they were going to be executed. But the guards cried and said they couldn't go through with it and just left them there. Jimmy admitted that he hadn't been right in the head ever since that day.

Jimmy wasn't at his window that day, so I was the only one out there, watching, swinging back and forward, back and forward. It was early in the afternoon on a warm, sunny Thursday in July, well into the school holidays. Nothing was happening on the street. The only noises to disturb the quiet of the place were the little squeaks that came intermittently from the gate. If Mum heard that squeaking, she would come to the front door and shout at me, telling me again to get off the gate, not to break it. But I was pretty certain that Mum wouldn't appear at the front door; not that afternoon, anyway. She was at the back of the house just then, in the kitchen with the two youngest children – 'the bairns', everyone calls them – and Dad. The last time I saw her, which was only ten minutes ago, she was sitting at the kitchen table, cradling Dad's head, trying to console him, trying to soothe the awful, relentless pain that was racking him.

The poor man had toothache; not the grinding, throbbing kind of toothache that people usually suffer, but a blinding, raging toothache that had come in the night and was now rampaging through the whole of his bottom jaw, making him want to cry out and beat his head against the wall. What made things even more tragic was that Dad couldn't get any treatment for the toothache. He had no money to pay the local dentist. He couldn't even scrape together the bus fare to go to the Dental Hospital in Edinburgh, where he would be treated for free. It was pay day at the dockyard the next day, another twenty-four hours before he would have the money, an eternity away.

The situation was hopeless, I had concluded, which was why I had sought solace out there. I couldn't bear to watch Dad's agony any longer, to hear the man groan and whimper. My sisters must have felt the same way; all three of them seemed to have cleared off, leaving just the bairns in the house and me swinging on the gate. A hopeless situation, I concluded again, continuing to swing back and forward, back and forward, feeling very depressed.

She appeared beside me as if from nowhere, startling me. It

was one of my sisters – 'the Mary one', as Mum often calls her. She was two years younger than me. She must have been lurking in the back yard and then sneaked round the side of the house.

'What do you want?' I asked, sounding annoyed.

She pushed the gate hard, forcing me to jump off it. Stepping quickly past me, she pulled the gate hard this time, banging it shut.

'To get past,' she said from the pavement.

I felt a wave of anger course through me, but I resisted the urge to rise to her provocation. Instead, I opened the gate again, climbed on to it and resumed my swinging. I looked at her, expecting to see that sardonic grin, the one she usually showed when she got me angry. But there was no grin today. She seemed sad, her dark eyes large and mournful, her cheeks wet, as if she had been crying hard for a long time.

'It's just not fair,' she said, tears welling up in her eyes.

She was wearing a lilac cotton frock with a lilac belt round it, a lilac ribbon in her hair, short white socks and leather sandals that Mum had recently whitened. But the pretty clothes seemed out of place on her, too dainty and girlish. Her hair was long and raven-black and full of ringlets; not the kind of ringlets that women, Mum included, manufacture with curling tongs, but real ones, like those of a Gypsy. She had a long, pointed nose, also like that of a Gypsy – or a witch, if you were being unkind. Beneath the big, dark freckles that covered her face, her skin was sallow, almost yellow. Her scrawny arms and legs were covered in sores that were coloured purple from the iodine that Mum had applied to stop her picking at the scabs. Her teeth were also a sight: ragged and crooked and stained brown from the medicine that she took for her iron deficiency.

'You're not one of mine,' Mum says whenever Mary is in her bad books, which is often. 'You must have been left on the doorstep by the tinkers.'

'It's not fair,' Mary repeated. The tears were now rolling down her cheeks.

'What's not fair?' I asked, putting a foot on the ground and halting the gate's motion.

'It's Dad. I can't stand to see him like that. Mum said he needs to get all his bottom teeth pulled out. He needs twenty pounds to pay the dentist, she said. Twenty pounds! It's just not fair!' The tears were spilling onto her frock, staining it.

'I know,' I said glumly. 'But stop crying like a big bairn. There's nothing can be done about it.'

'Oh yes there is,' she sobbed.

She wiped away her tears with the backs of her hands and stormed off along the pavement.

'Where are you going?' I called after her.

She stopped and turned round.

'Nowhere,' she called back.

She made a face at me, stuck out her tongue and gave me the V-sign. Then she continued on her way.

'Come back here!' I demanded, feeling my anger rise again.

'Fuck off!' she shouted without stopping or even turning round.

My anger mounted.

'Bitch!' I cried.

I gripped the top of the gate for a few moments. Then I began to swing again, back and forward, back and forward, until she was out of sight and the anger was soothed away. She always did that to me; made me boil and do rash things and get into trouble. It was less than a fortnight before that she had gotten me into real hot water. It was a Saturday afternoon. I had been in the living room watching television when I saw Rob Lyle's van draw up outside. It isn't a van really, but an old bus that has been painted red and converted into a mobile shop. It sells fruit and vegetables and other groceries, as well as cigarettes and sweets. You can walk down the aisle of the bus. There are wooden shelves on both sides, where the seats used to be. When you climb onto the bus, there's always a big pile of potatoes at the top of the steps. Clods of earth still cling to the potatoes, and on wet days you have to squelch through mud to get past them.

Anyway, Mary appeared beside the van that afternoon. When she realised that I had spotted her, she waved to me, not to be friendly, but to show off the coin that she was holding in her hand. It was a two-bob bit or a half-crown. She had stolen it off someone somewhere, I was sure. She disappeared into the van, returning a minute or so later with a Mars Bar in her hand. Knowing that I was watching her, she stood in front of the house, unwrapped the top of the Mars Bar and commenced to lick it as if it was an ice-cream. Every lick was slow and exaggerated; her tongue stretched its full length, like a lizard's. I grew so angry that I rapped on the window and motioned to her to scram, but my fist went straight through the glass. It was only one of the smaller panes, but I got hell for it nevertheless.

I had calmed down after Mary's latest provocation. I was glad that I hadn't chased her along the street and done something I would have regretted. She was a real problem, though. She spat and swore and fought and lied all the time. And she was a thief. Everyone in the house had learned from bitter experience to keep their money hidden well away from her, otherwise it just disappeared. I remember the time Mum actually watched Mary take money out of her purse. When she was confronted about the theft, Mary looked Mum straight in the face and swore blind that she was innocent. Depriving her of television or confining her to her room didn't have any effect on her. No amount of skelping would change her either. She seemed compelled to do the things she did. I didn't behave like her, nor did my other two sisters. Everyone said she was the black sheep of the family. Another hopeless situation, I sighed. My thoughts returned quickly to Dad's plight back there in the kitchen. I swung on the gate, back and forward, back and forward, feeling even more depressed.

I saw her coming back along the street. She had been away for only twenty minutes. I got off the gate and closed it to make sure that she couldn't do the same thing to me twice. As she came closer, I saw that she was smiling, showing her stained teeth.

'What are you looking so pleased about?' I asked. I deliberately kept the gate closed to bar her way.

Out of a pocket at the side of her frock, she took a piece of paper. It looked like it had been folded many times.

'Look,' she said. 'See what I found.'

She unfolded the paper and flattened it out to reveal a crisp, new Bank of England twenty-pound note.

My mouth fell open.

'Where did you get that?' I gasped.

She shrugged her shoulders.

'I found it,' she said. 'On the pavement back there. I was just walking along, and there it was. Twenty pounds. Just what Dad needs...'

I knew she was lying, but it didn't matter. I opened the gate wide to let her pass. Mary ran into the house, leaving the front door open. Only moments later, she reappeared at the door with Mum and Dad. Dad had a big woollen scarf wrapped tightly round his jaw. He was hugging Mary.

'You're a wee angel, hen,' he mumbled from behind the scarf.

Then he came down the front steps and strode through the gate on his way to the dentist, ruffling my hair as he passed. I looked up at Mary. Framed by the door, snuggled into Mum's side, she was smiling sweetly, as if butter wouldn't melt in her mouth.

Chapter Nine
The Big Garden

Yes, a story with a happy ending for a change. But it just goes to prove that there was never enough money in the house. At one point, Dad started to do people's gardens in the evenings and at weekends in order to earn extra cash. And he was pretty good at it. He worked locally to begin with and then further afield as his reputation spread. I used to help him when I was a bit younger. The last time was when we did the big garden at that posh house in Edinburgh. That was another day to remember, but one without such a happy ending – for me, anyway.

It was to be a day of firsts for me. For the first time, I would ride alone on the bus to Edinburgh. Although I would be getting off the bus quite a bit before the city centre, that first journey on my own was still a big step for a twelve year-old from the sticks. For the first time, too, I was to be paid for the work I would do that day; not like the odd sixpence or shilling that I received from Dad for helping him round the Ferry, but a proper hourly rate direct from the owner. Well, that's how Dad explained it.

So it was that early on a Saturday in mid-April we set off from home on our respective journeys. Our destination was the wealthy suburb of Barnton, about five miles to the east of the Ferry.

I would get there by bus. Dad, wanting to save on bus fares, would cycle there. As I left the house and headed left to get to the bus stop on the High Street, Dad gave his customary 'Cheery bye' and pedalled off in the opposite direction on the old boneshaker with peeling black paint that he had 'borrowed' from the dockyard. Even when I had reached the end of our street and Dad had disappeared round the opposite corner, I could still hear his happy whistle. As if to bless our mission, a soft Spring sun came out that morning and continued to shine all day.

    I don't remember much about the bus journey, except that I spent most of its fifteen minutes fighting off waves of nausea. I had never been a good bus traveller. When I was five, I had gone with Dad on my first bus trip into Edinburgh. We had barely stepped off the bus in Charlotte Square when I unloaded my stomach down the pinstriped trouser leg of a passing businessman. Dad had been highly embarrassed, but the man had been very kind, even patting me on the head and giving me a sixpence before he continued on his way. On bus journeys after that, I was made to sit on a newspaper: to reduce the vibrations, I was told. There was no newspaper to sit on during that latest journey, though; nothing to lessen the constant shuddering. That, combined with the frequent juddering stops and starts, and the occasional pungent whiffs of petrol, kept my stomach in turmoil, forcing me to breathe in and out slowly and to concentrate on anything other than being on a smelly, slow-moving bus. It was of no surprise, therefore, that when the bus pulled up in front of the Barnton Hotel, the bus stop where Dad and I had agreed to meet, I had no idea if it had passed Dad on its route.

    As I waited my turn to climb down from the bus into the fresh air, I felt both relief and anxiety: immense relief for not having been sick, of course, but the beginnings of anxiety about meeting up with Dad. He said that the bus might get there before him. If that was the case, I should wait at the bus stop. But what if something had gone wrong? What if he had had an accident? Or his bike had broken down? How long was I to wait? With these thoughts forming in my mind, my heart skipped a beat when I couldn't see Dad at first glance. Then I recognised his old bike. It was just a few feet to the left of the bus stop, propped up against a low wall. Behind the wall was the sombre Victorian façade of the Barnton Hotel. And there, sitting on the wall next to the bike, grinning and waving to me, was Dad.

    He was wearing his working clothes: a pair of dark trousers tucked into short Wellingtons; the long dark jacket from an ancient suit; an old white collarless shirt; and that red kerchief knotted round his neck. A black beret with a narrow leather trim, placed at an angle on his head, finished off the outfit. With his dark stubble making him look more swarthy than usual, his long, slightly hooked nose, and a freshly lit roll-up dangling from a corner of his mouth, he could easily have been a member of the French Resistance. But he wasn't. He was just my Dad.

    Soon, we were well away from the noisy traffic on Queensferry Road, having turned a corner into the quiet cul-de-sac at the rear of the Barnton Hotel, Dad wheeling his bike along the pavement and me walking quickly beside him, striving to keep up. There was a wood across the road on our left and a row of big houses immediately to our right. Every house in the row was designed in a different style. A few were semi-detached, but most were detached, standing in their own grounds and fronted by wide gardens or courtyards.

'The job today is a really special one,' Dad was saying. 'It's for a high-ranking Navy officer from the base. The head gaffer at the dockyard gave him my name.'

He seemed very proud that his reputation had been passed on at such a high level.

I had been busy studying the rich men's houses ahead of us, but now I looked up at Dad.

'Is he an Admiral, then?' I asked, catching my breath.

Dad grinned and shook his head.

'No,' he said. 'Not yet, anyway. No, he's just a Commander, son.'

We stopped in front of the last but one house in the cul-de-sac. It was a large, whitewashed affair with a built-in double garage on the left; enormous, rounded bay windows on either side of a porticoed front door; and a courtyard that was completely paved. A sleek, modern caravan squatted under a clump of trees in one corner of the otherwise bare courtyard; bare, that is, except for the weeds – grass and dandelions, mostly – that sprouted almost everywhere in the spaces between the paving stones.

Dad tutted at the sight of the weeds. With me hurrying behind him, he ignored the front door and crossed over the courtyard to follow a path round the right-hand side of the house. There, at the farther end, he stopped, took off his beret and knocked at another, smaller door. The door was opened by a wispy woman in a cashmere twinset and matching skirt. I don't recall much more about the woman's appearance, except that her eyes were grey and cold and that she looked a good bit older than Mum. And there was that voice, of course; a voice that could have cut glass.

'Yes?' it said loudly and haughtily, more of a statement than a question.

Nor do I recall much about the ensuing conversation between Dad and her. Standing back from them, I had caught sight of the garden at the rear of the house: a wide expanse of lawn, which was lined on both sides by shrub and flower beds, and which seemed to stretch for ages down to a copse of trees. It wasn't the sheer size of the garden that had grabbed my attention, though, but its condition. Between large patches of clover and clumps of dandelions on the lawn, the grass was over a foot high. Weeds of all descriptions, some as tall as the tallest shrubs, also thronged along the borders.

I found myself comparing this cavernous place – with its cracked and peeling whitewash, its weed-strewn courtyard and its unkempt garden – and the much tinier semi-detached house that we rented from the Council. Our back garden wasn't large and rolling, but we made maximum use of its limited space. There was a small drying green with a neat concrete border. There was a patch given over to growing vegetables: potatoes mostly, but also carrots, leeks, onions, cabbage and lettuce. There was a trellis for growing peas, a rhubarb patch and even a small patch of wild strawberries. There was also a row of blackcurrant bushes and another of gooseberry bushes, from which Mum made jam. The border along the side of the house was always full of shrubs and flowers. The borders round the lawn in our front garden were similarly chock-a-block. The lawn itself had been laid by Dad a couple of years before with squares of turf he had cut from the soft grass that grew below bushes in the little wood close to our home. The wild climbing rose bushes, which Mum had planted to hide the Council's ugly chain link fence at the front of the house, and which bloomed white and yellow and pink all summer, had also come from the wood; like the turf, snatched at dusk when no-one was about. Yes, what little we had was nurtured, treasured, precious. The people who lived there were the opposite; they had everything – too much, perhaps – and they seemed not to care about any of it.

A sudden rising of her voice brought my attention back to the woman.

'Do, please, make use of whatever, um, implements are in there,' she was saying, waving her hand dismissively at the small garden hut behind us. There was a look of disgust on her face, as if the hut contained the plague.

She began to close the door, but paused.

'Oh, yes,' she said, not looking at either of us, 'I'll be preparing a spot of lunch for you and the, um, boy. About one o'clock. I'll call you ten minutes before so that you can, um, wash up and things.'

There was an awkward silence as Dad looked first at his watch and then at me, and finally checked his jacket pockets nervously.

'Thanks very much,' he said eventually, smiling.

But I sensed the disappointment behind that smile. Both he and I had been looking forward to the pile of sandwiches that Mum had made for us just before we left. Some were made of cheese, others of egg and a few of my favourite, corned beef. They had been neatly parcelled up in the greaseproof wrapper that came with the loaf of bread, and were now weighing down the left-hand pocket of Dad's jacket. Acting as a counterbalance, a big flask of tea, already milked and sugared, stuck out of the right-hand pocket. Instead of enjoying our sandwiches and tea in the Spring sunshine, it looked like we would have to endure a posh lunch in a posh house in the company of a very posh woman. When the door closed behind the woman, Dad and I stood looking at each other for some moments. Then we shrugged in unison.

With only the occasional word exchanged between us, we worked solidly throughout the rest of the morning. Dad found a small sickle in the hut and a sharpening tool. The tool was made of steel and had a rough surface; slender and tapered, it looked like a dagger without a hilt. The hut also contained one of those newfangled electric lawn mowers. Dad seemed dismayed when he saw the contraption, but his eyes lit up when he spied a manual mower beside it. The older machine was bigger and wider, and came equipped with a heavy steel roller. I had seen one like it being used on the Bowling Green back in the Ferry. Dad was almost gleeful as he dragged the machine out of the hut.

'That'll do nicely,' he said.

Once Dad had sharpened the sickle, he set about cutting down the long grass on the lawn. My job was to gather up the fallen grass and transport it by wheelbarrow to the compost heap under the trees at the foot of the garden. After that, Dad gave me the sharpening tool and showed me how to use it to burrow deep into the lawn so that I could loosen and then pull up the roots of the biggest dandelion plants. He also showed me how to pack the resultant holes with earth and little stones. Between us, we prepared the lawn for its first proper cut in a long time.

Dad had just wheeled the mower into place at the top of the lawn, and I had begun to haul some of the larger weeds out of one of the shrub beds, when we heard her.

'Cooee!' she cried.

Wearing a white apron now, she was waving to us from outside the same door at the side of the house.

'Cooee!' she cried again.

'Fuck!' I heard Dad say under his breath.

He looked over at me and sighed. Tiny bits of grass mingled with the sweat that ran down his temples.

After taking off our shoes outside, we followed the woman through the door and straight into the kitchen. For such a grand house, its kitchen seemed rather small and nondescript. A tall fridge occupied the corner facing us as we entered the room. Next to the fridge was a round table with a yellow Formica top. Four aluminium chairs with yellow plastic seats were spaced around the table. I noticed that places had been set at only two of the chairs, a knife and fork, a napkin and a beaker of water in each case. Along the wall to the right of the table and chairs was a door leading into the rest of the house, a cooker and a large cupboard. On the adjacent wall was a long, narrow window that overlooked the back garden. Below the window was a smaller cupboard, also with a yellow Formica top, a draining board and a sink. A geyser protruded from the wall just to the right of the window, its arm hovering over one end of the sink.

The woman motioned towards the sink, handing Dad a towel and a bar of soap.

'You can wash up there,' she said.

Dad and I took turns to wash our hands and faces before sitting down at the table. The woman busied herself at the cooker. She spoke with her back to us.

'It's always the way, isn't it? The lady who, um, cooks and cleans for us isn't here today. So you'll just have to, um, put up with my efforts.'

She turned round with a plate in each hand.

'I've heated up what was left over from last night's meal and, um, divided it between you,' she continued. 'I do hope you'll enjoy.'

As she placed the plates in front of us, Dad muttered his thanks. I echoed his mutter. The woman stood behind us for some seconds, seeming to hesitate.

Finally she said, 'The Commander's away at the moment... exercises, I think... in the, um, Med. But I think he'd be rather pleased with the, um, progress you're making today. I wonder, though, if you would remember to do something about the front of the house... the, um, courtyard... those ghastly weeds, you know...'

Probably certain that she couldn't see the expression on his face, Dad looked at me, smiled wryly and rolled his eyes.

'Aye, no problem,' he said lightly without turning his head, 'we'll not forget.'

'Jolly good,' acknowledged the woman.

She appeared to hesitate again. Then she looked at me for the first time that day, catching my eye. She smiled weakly.

'I have two sons, you know. A bit older than you. They're off at boarding school just now. But they'll be back in the, um, Summer.'

I couldn't think of anything to say in reply.

'Yes,' I managed to mumble.

'Anyway, enjoy your lunch,' she said and promptly left the room, closing the door behind her.

Just for a moment I felt sorry for the woman, all alone in her big house, her husband and her sons God knows how many miles away. But the feeling passed in an instant, replaced by the memory of her coldness.

We examined our plates as soon as she had gone. Each plate contained one slice of meat that looked like roast pork, three small boiled potatoes and two Brussels sprouts.

'It was hardly worth washing our hands for,' I hissed.

'Shush now,' Dad whispered, but I knew he felt the same.

As if we had rehearsed it, we picked up our knives and forks simultaneously and looked again at the Brussels sprouts on our plates. Dad groaned and I went 'Yuk!' It looked like we would get to eat Mum's sandwiches after all.

Outside in the sunshine with our shoes back on, Dad handed me the sharpening tool again.

'I'm sorry, son,' he said, 'but I need a favour from you. Would you mind doing the weeds at the front? The Commander never mentioned the front, and we won't get finished today if I try and do it myself. I ken it's bloody awful work, son, but just do your best, eh?'

'Sure, Dad,' I replied. 'I'll give it a go.'

Although the words were said stoically, secretly I was glad to have been given the responsibility, to have the whole courtyard to myself.

We worked on for the next couple of hours, Dad at the rear, pushing the heavy mower down and then back up the lawn, and me at the front on my hands and knees, picking out the weeds from between the paving stones. Around three o'clock, we stopped for a break. Out of sight from the house, we sat among the trees at the foot of the lawn, eating our sandwiches and drinking our tea. While Dad rested his back against the trunk of a tree, stretched out his legs and began to make a roll-up, I went for a pee behind one of the other trees. Dad followed suit shortly afterwards, with me keeping lookout for him. Not having been invited by the woman to do so, neither of us had wanted to go to the house to ask to use the toilet.

It was when I was returning to the courtyard to resume my work that I stopped at the window on the side of the house. The window was next to the door that we had used to go into the kitchen. I had gone straight past it several times now, but this time curiosity got the better of me. I wanted to take just a peek inside, to gain a tiny inkling of how the people in that big house lived. But the room behind the window was disappointingly small and narrow. On the wall opposite me, I saw a door on the left and a pair of bunk beds on the right. A cricket bat rested against the wall at the side of the door. Her two boys, I concluded. Their bedroom. There were no pictures or posters on the walls, though, no Airfix models suspended from the ceiling, nothing to brighten up the room, which seemed drab and impersonal and uncared for. On the top of what could have been a sideboard or a bookcase directly below the window, I could see a pile of old comics and a shallow fruit bowl, in which someone had placed a rugby ball. Next to the bowl, as if just discarded there, was a small, slim, lozenge-shaped tin of toffees. The tin was silver-grey with a picture of a racing car on the lid. I had seen tins just like it the previous Christmas in McGillivary's sweetshop back home. A posh boy's unwanted stocking filler, I remember thinking.

At six o'clock, the sun was sinking below the roof line at the front of the house, leaving a chilly shadow in its place. Having deposited the last of the weeds and muck from the courtyard on the compost heap at the rear, I returned to collect my jacket and the sharpening tool. My back was aching, my knees were sore and the constant wielding of the rough handle of the tool had left me with blisters on both hands. But I was happy, pleased with myself and with the work I had done. The courtyard was immaculate now. Dad had said so, too, when he came round earlier to view my handiwork.

I put on my jacket and went back round the side of the house, where Dad was putting on his own jacket. After returning the tool to the hut and closing the hut door, I took one last look at the garden. Its whole length was bathed in a soft orange glow from the rays of the setting sun. Neatly clipped and freshly edged, the lawn was now unblemished. Dad had even managed to create that two-tone effect with the mower, just like on football pitches and cricket grounds that you saw on the television. The plants along the borders also now looked healthy and vibrant and weed-free. The many months of neglect seemed to have just vanished.

'Magnificent,' I said, standing alongside Dad.

'Aye,' Dad nodded. 'A professional job, right enough.'

Clutching both his beret and the handlebars of his bike in his left hand, Dad knocked at the kitchen door with his right. As soon as the woman appeared at the door, he said, 'That's us finished now and ready to go.'

Still wearing the white apron, the woman stepped out of the house to look down over the garden, just as we had done moments before. Then turning back to face us, she exclaimed with her hands clasped, 'Absolutely marvellous! The Commander will be delighted!' Her voice was more strident than ever.

She produced a small manila envelope from the pocket in the front of her apron. Handing the envelope to Dad, she said, 'For, um, ten hours' work. As agreed with the Commander. And thank you so much.'

'It's a pleasure,' Dad replied, slipping the envelope, unopened, into the inside pocket of his jacket.

The woman looked at me now, smiled and dug something else out of her apron pocket.

'And this is for you, young man,' she said, bending to offer the object to me. 'Thank you ever so much.'

My heart sank when I recognised the tin and the picture of the racing car on it. I took the tin from her and slid it into my jacket pocket. I didn't want to look at the woman, so I kept my eyes lowered and said 'Thank you' to her as politely as I could, just as I had been taught at home. I was crestfallen, but I tried hard to remain impassive, to fight back the tears that were welling up in my eyes. When I looked up at Dad, I could see from his face that he, too, was deeply disappointed.

With the woman's false 'Byee' ringing in our ears, we left that big house the same way we had arrived, Dad wheeling his bike along the pavement and me walking quickly to keep up with him. There seemed to be an added urgency in our step this time, though, as if we wanted to be rid of the place as quickly as possible.

We didn't speak a word until we reached the bus stop on the other side of Queensferry Road. By that time, the surprise and disappointment that I had experienced back at the house had hardened into a sullen anger.

Dad put on his beret.

'Look,' he said, 'I don't have any lights on my bike, and I want to get home before it's dark, so I'm going to push off just now. The bus should be here in about ten minutes.'

He paused, searching my face.

'You did a great job today, son. And I wouldn't have got on

so well without you. I'm really sorry about that bloody woman and her bastard sweeties. Don't worry about getting paid, though. I'll square up with you when you get home.'

I could feel the tears building up again. I tried to smile.

'Okay,' I said hoarsely, 'I'll see you soon.'

Dad looked tired and gaunt. There was no cheery whistle this time as he mounted his bike and pedalled off slowly into the stream of northbound traffic.

I was still angry when Dad left. Ten minutes passed. Then twenty. My anger was mounting. My eyes were beginning to hurt from constantly peering up the road to check for the shape of the bus in the distance. The traffic going both ways seemed to have grown in volume and speed and noise. Alone at the bus stop, I felt small and insignificant in the midst of the cacophony. The sun had gone now, and the whole place had become colder and unfriendly.

After half an hour, the anger had gone, no longer important. I was very worried now. And there was no-one to talk to, no-one to share my concerns with. But those concerns simply melted away when I saw the bus approaching at last. Trying to stand as tall as possible, I stuck out my hand as straight and as far as I could. My heart sank for the second time that day when the bus sped past me, its driver not even acknowledging my presence. I caught a glimpse of people standing in the aisle of the bus, some staring at me as they flashed by.

Every instinct I possessed wanted me to panic at that moment, but something familiar about the packed bus made me think instead. Then it dawned on me. It was Saturday evening, of course! The time when the city's outsiders finished their shopping and wanted to return home. There were always long queues at the

Bus Station at this time, and the buses were always late and full and too few. I had been a member of that same exodus on several occasions. I knew that once the buses left the Bus Station it was rare for any of their passengers to get off before the first stop in the Ferry, leaving no room for new passengers to get on along the route out of the city. If I continued to wait there at the bus stop, there was no guarantee that I would get on the next bus or the one after that or even the one after that.

When I realised that it would be better to walk home, I was glad. It meant no more waiting and uncertainty, and no more disappointments as buses flew past me. Almost as important, it meant that the morning's experience would not be repeated; there would be no more fear of being sick on the bus. Moreover, by cutting down through Dalmeny village, I could take a quicker route than the bus. I could be home in an hour, an hour and a half at most.

'Who needs buses anyway?' I said to myself as I set off positively at a brisk pace.

My positive outlook didn't last long. As I walked, the events of that evening replayed in my head, and my anger and resentment returned. I was angry with the bus service for its inadequacy. I was angry with Dad for being too soft, for accepting what the woman did without complaint. Most of all, I was angry with the woman. Dad didn't check inside the envelope, but I knew that she hadn't paid him for my work. She had cheated me out of ten hours' payment. She had then belittled my efforts, adding insult to injury by presenting me with something that was of no value either to her or to her own children. She may not have done any of this deliberately or with malice, but it wasn't an excuse to be thoughtless and arrogant. To make it all worse, Dad said he would square up with me, but that would be like stealing from him.

These angry thoughts consumed me so much that I didn't realise how fast I had been walking. Before I knew it, I was crossing Cramond Bridge. Out of breath and with the traffic thundering past, I stopped for a rest, leaning over the parapet to watch the shallow, fast-moving waters of the River Almond far below. I heard a soft clunk as the tin of toffees in my jacket knocked against the parapet wall. I took the tin out of my pocket and, without hesitation, hurled it over the wall as hard as I could. The tin made a long arc before plummeting. I saw a glint as it skiffed off a flat stone at the side of the river and then a splash as it hit the water, immediately disappearing below the surface. Sparkling in the twilight, undisturbed by this little drama, the Almond continued to gurgle on its journey down to the sea.

It was at that moment, when the offending tin had gone for ever, that I made the vow. I would never end up like Dad, labouring all day at the dockyard and then spending every spare hour doing people's gardens, always striving to pick up that few extra quid to feed and clothe his big family. I had brains and intelligence, so everyone kept telling me. If those failed to make enough money, I would lie and cheat and steal if I had to. But, whatever happened, I would never, ever rely on handouts from her kind again. Thus resolved, I resumed my journey home with a fresh vigour.

The dusk light was fading when I turned the corner into our street. High above the trees of the little wood at the end of the street, a flock of starlings was wheeling across the darkening sky. I could see Dad standing at the top of the steps outside our front door. He was in his shirt sleeves, a mug of tea in one hand and a roll-up in the other. He waved when he saw me, and I waved back.

'The bus was full, so I walked,' I said as I shut the garden gate behind me.

Dad nodded.

'Thought so,' he smiled.

When I reached the top of the steps, he put his arm round my shoulders and led me into the house.

'Come on,' he said, 'I owe you some money.'

He never mentioned the tin of toffees again. Nor did I.

Oh, Dad, if only you could be standing on top of the steps when I get back this evening! Then you could put your arm round me again and tell me that everything's all right. But that's not going to happen, is it? Oh, Dad…

Chapter Ten

A Runner for the Bookie

Christ, I've got to stop behaving like a kid and thinking that way! I should be thinking instead about the next bit of Dad's story before I run out of time. I don't want to forget the other way that he tried to make more money: his job as a runner for the bookie.

He worked for P. Percy & Son, Bookmakers, on the High Street, collecting bets from the men he worked with in the dockyard, as well as from people's houses near us. I used to go out with him to the houses on a Saturday morning, so I got to know his round. Which was just as well, because I was able to stand in for him when he became ill.

Collecting bets inside the dockyard was illegal, of course. One time Dad was caught by the dockyard police. He was angry and hurt about that; not so much because they confiscated his bets, but because someone had obviously snitched on him. People can be bastards, can't they? But Dad bounced back. Before leaving the dockyard after his shift, he began to rewrite the bets on a piece of till roll, which he would then wrap up into a tight, little wad and stick under his tongue. He was strip-searched twice by the dockyard police, but they didn't find anything. They left him alone after that. Dad felt really proud for outfoxing them and beating the snitcher.

Dad did his own fair share of betting on the horses, of course. His bets were always small, though, just like the ones he collected from the men in the dockyard. He said once that him and those men were all losers.

'We're wee men, betting a few coppers at a time,' he told me. 'If we win one week, the bookies take it back the next. There's only one way to beat the bastards. You need to watch out for the young horses with potential. And you need to follow their progress; to build up a system, so that you know what circumstances suit them and the right time to bet on them. Most of all, you need money – big money – that you're prepared to gamble and lose. That's the way the real gamblers – the big winners – do it. And there's not many of them in the Ferry, son.'

A good system and plenty of money: those were the secrets, according to Dad. His own system had been coming along. He had already picked out about fifty promising horses. Regularly and painstakingly, he had been recording their form on cards that he kept in a little red box at home. He took that box into the hospital with him. Would you believe it? He thought he was going in for a rest! Anyway, getting big money to put on those horses was a different thing altogether. It was only when he was actually in the hospital that he managed to do it – just that once, and then see what happened...

But I'll get to that soon enough. In the meantime, while I'm on the subject of Dad trying to make more money, there's his big promotion to remember. He went from being just an ordinary labourer at the dockyard to being in charge of maintaining the sewage system for the whole base.

'Your Dad's been promoted from shit shoveller to chief shit

shoveller,' was how Mum described it at the time. She said later that she had only been joking, but we all knew that she was being sarcastic. Bitch!

Even that bit of good fortune for Dad didn't come without its problems. Instead of passing on to Dad his copy of the sewage plans for the base, which showed the locations of all the manholes and the like, Mr McLucas, the old man from round the corner whose job Dad got when he retired, tore up the plans. It meant that Dad had to go to the dockyard bosses and ask to borrow the master plans. Then he bought some graph paper and coloured pencils and go me to copy the plans. That was some job, and all because of that miserable old bastard, McLucas. Dad couldn't fathom out why he did what he did, whether it was out of jealousy or just plain spite. I don't know either, but I wouldn't be surprised if he was the same one who snitched on Dad to the dockyard police. Mum's pretty sure that that's the case. You know, it's not fucking fair! Dad's dead, but he's still alive, strolling around the streets arm-in-arm with his wife and looking all smug. Right now, I'd like to stick a knife in his scrawny gizzard!

God, that's me getting angry again. And I don't want to do that. I want to keep on with Dad's story. I'm getting to the root of all his problems now. Money! None of the extra cash that Dad got from his promotion, the runner's job and doing gardens made any difference at all. Mum was still buying on tick; the debt wasn't shifting. It was just like that little statue of Andy Capp; it was 'Rent Spent' right enough.

Chapter Eleven
The Bad Times

Oh, God, I've got that horrible, empty feeling in the pit of my stomach again. I wish the bus could turn round right here and take me home. I've just realised that it has already gone through both Broxburn and Uphall without me noticing. It's at Dechmont junction now, waiting to join the traffic on the A8. Then it'll have a straight run through to St Mary's. And in a few moments it'll be passing the entrance to the grounds of Bangour Hospital, where Dad's story came to an end. So how come his story did end in that godforsaken place over there behind the trees? How come Dad had to perish in a decrepit, little hospital in the middle of nowhere, next door to a fucking loony bin?

    The bad times seemed to come quickly, without any warning, and then build to a head in a short time. It was probably when Dad had his pocket picked last year that they began. After collecting the returns from the bookies early one Saturday evening, he had gone to the pub. When he came out of it a few hours later, the money was gone. Dad was devastated by that. I remember him crying in the house afterwards. He was going to have to borrow money in order to pay out the returns from his own pocket. Mum said that he had been stupid with drink, but Dad denied it. He suspected that it was

Pigeon Maudsley who picked his pocket, but he couldn't be sure. Mum calls Pigeon Maudsley 'a young thug and a bully'. I've seen him around. He's a big galoot with a ruddy complexion and one of those Tony Curtis hairstyles. According to Mum, him and his pals are always larking about and getting into fights. Well, Pigeon Maudsley, I promise you now that once I'm a bit older I'm going to come and find you and wipe that smirk off your big red face!

But it wasn't just him who stole from Dad. Mum was a much bigger thief. She couldn't hide from the tallymen any longer; they were finally catching up with her and hounding her for money. So, without telling Dad, she would 'borrow' from the returns that he kept in the house until he was able to pay them out. When Dad realised what was going on, he started putting the returns in a little vanity case, which he kept locked. That didn't deter her, though; she just forced the lock. Then he began to hide the vanity case at the back of the coal cellar, behind all the rubbish in there. That didn't stop her either; she found the hiding place eventually, broke into the case again and practically emptied it. I can still see that look of utter dejection on Dad's face when he discovered what she had done.

Not surprisingly, Mum's pilfering led to lots of rows about money between her and Dad. The rows became more frequent and louder until there was a shouting match nearly every night of the week. They usually took place in the living room after Dad had eaten his tea, while us kids stayed out of the way in the kitchen. Then one night last winter the row spread out into the hall. Dad finally snapped when he found out that Mum had taken on even more tick. He had her pinned down on the floor of the hall with his hands round her neck when I rushed to her aid.

'Leave her alone, you bastard!' I shouted at him before

jumping on his back and pulling him off Mum.

Shouting that at him was just a reflex, I suppose, but I know that I'm going to regret having done it for the rest of my life. He got up immediately, put his coat on and left the house. Some of us went out to the pictures later that night. We passed Dad as he was coming up the steps of the Back Braes on his way home. He looked cold and lonely and hurt; he was like a broken man. I didn't enjoy the pictures after seeing him that way.

And then, of course, there was the unspoken business of Mum carrying on with other men. During the day, while Dad was away at work, she had a habit of inviting the street vendors to come in for a cup of tea. It was purely innocent most of the time, but in some cases there was a bit more to it. There was that big brute, Stan, who used to drive the baker's van, for example; he was forever touching Mum. And there's that other brute, Rob Lyle. He comes along the street every day in his mobile shop. One afternoon, I came home to actually see him at the top of our stairs. There's no toilet upstairs, so what reason did he have for being there? There was *definitely* something going on between Mum and him. His wife, Mae, had a black eye not that long ago. The rumour was that Rob gave it to her when she accused him of having an affair with Mum. The woman still stares daggers whenever she sees any of us; I'm sure she hates us.

Although we children knew about Mum carrying on like that, nothing was ever said between us. But the thing is that if we knew, the neighbours knew and, the Ferry being the way it is, Dad was bound to know as well. That must have made him feel ten times worse. Sometimes I think that I should have let him strangle her that night…

So with her carrying on behind his back in addition to building up the debt and stealing the returns, and with him working all hours and worrying about money and having a constant knot in his stomach, it was no wonder that he became ill. It was only a small ulcer to begin with, or so he was told by the doctors. They seemed to dismiss it and just gave him tablets to take. They also told him to change his diet by cutting out fried food and eating lots of fish cooked in milk, which Dad hated. None of it helped, though; the pain got worse. Then the doctors gave him stronger tablets, but they didn't work either. Dad became a different man; he was always tired and grey-looking – and quiet as well, as if he had retreated into himself. And he was doubled up in pain most of the time. It got so bad that he stopped doing people's gardens and I started collecting bets round the local streets to help him with his runner's job. At lunchtimes, he used to cycle from the dockyard up the road to Nana's house so that he could lie on her couch for half-an-hour. We only found that out from Nana after the funeral. She said that Dad had kept it from Mum so as not to worry her.

Then the doctors finally recognised that Dad was really ill and agreed to send him into hospital for tests. I waited at the bus stop with him the morning he went into Bangour. He was dressed up in his suit and carrying that little brown suitcase. He looked peaceful, not worried at all...

Fuck! The tears are welling up again. I'm going to have to compose myself in order to get through the one last bit of Dad's story before we get to Bathgate. It's the final episode: the tale of when Dad became the Aga Khan and won and lost at the same time. It's the tale that summed up his life.

Chapter Twelve
The Aga Khan

The details are still vivid in my mind. I can see that little shop perched on the end of the terrace overlooking the High Street. The whole of its frontage – even the glass of the single display window and the extractor fan in the centre of the glass – is painted a dull, anonymous shade of yellow. The paintwork is peeling and flaking in places. Above the door and window, big brown letters stretch the length of the shop, proclaiming to the town: P. PERCY & SON, BOOKMAKERS.

And I can see me hesitating outside the open doorway. The late June sunshine was warm on my face that afternoon. I can even remember smelling the freshness of the soft breeze that was carried up to me from the sea. Down below in the narrow High Street, local shoppers jostled with talkative, slow-moving visitors to create that familiar Saturday buzz. I glanced along the terrace and up at the Jubilee clock. It was nearly two o'clock, still a good half-hour before the first race. I checked my jacket pockets again, feeling for the wad of crumpled slips on the left and the reassuring weight of coins and notes on the right. Then I left the sunshine and stepped into the shop.

The sensation was at once fascinating and unnerving: the

sudden transportation from the brightness and freshness and cheerfulness of the day into an alien, uncharted territory of stale air, hushed voices and permanent dimness. As my eyes adjusted to the gloom, I could see that the walls and ceiling of the room were painted the same dull yellow as the shop front. A single pendant hung from the middle of the ceiling, its bare bulb casting a weak, shadowy light across the room. The floorboards were also bare, but brightened here and there by splashes of gold from sunbeams that glanced through paint cracks in the window. Narrow, chest-high plywood ledges ran along the walls to my left and right. On the wall facing me, there was a door to the left and a small, glass-fronted hatch in the centre. The hatch gave a glimpse of the more intense light in the office behind it. Above it, the metallic voice of a woman droned through a big Tannoy speaker; in a detached, tinny monotone, she was announcing the latest starting prices from the courses.

    I walked towards the hatch. Men were standing at the ledges. Some were leaning casually, smoking, quietly studying the race cards that were pinned to the wall in front of them. Others were hunched over the ledges, deep in concentration, printing out with meticulous effort the exotic names of their chosen runners; sometimes pausing, checking, their biros poised over their little works of craftsmanship. I trod softly past the men. I noticed that the pens they were using were attached to the wall with pieces of string. I stood at the hatch, sweeping back my hair from my forehead, feeling suddenly awkward. I knew that my cheeks were beginning to glow from the redness that always came with my self-consciousness. I felt like an intruder in that place where real men gathered to carry out men's business. And yet I could sense no excitement or adventure in the dingy room; the men's actions seemed so furtive, so seamy.

The face at the hatch was round and pink and chubby, like a cherub's. The man's eyes were small, and his hair was biscuit-coloured and wispy. The voice coming through the glass sounded distant and impersonal.

'I'm sorry, son, you can't place a bet here.'

My cheeks were burning now. I stammered, 'My Dad sent me... Derry...'

'Och, it's Derry's son,' the man smiled, but the smile seemed more like a leer. 'Come right through the back, son. You're alright.'

Still acutely nervous, I stepped over to the door on my left. My hand fumbled on the doorknob. Then I opened the door and went into the tiny office. The smell of stale cigar smoke was overpowering. In less time than it took to look round the office, the two Alsatians had slid forward. They looked like twins: both young and light-coloured, and thin to the point of emaciation. The dogs didn't bark or growl or snarl; they just crouched on either side of me, their hungry eyes fixed on mine, daring me to move. I kept my arms rigid at my sides. My eyes were opened wide with fright. My blush had vanished.

'Sheba! Shona! Back!'

The dogs retreated immediately to flop down at the feet of the man who had given the commands. The man was dumpy and dapper and in his fifties. He was sitting on a swivel chair with his back to a battered roll-top desk. Thin strands of silvery hair were Brylcreemed back over his pointed head. He wore a white shirt with mother-of-pearl cuff links, a striped tie, patterned braces, sharply creased pinstripe trousers and very shiny black shoes. In the glare of the anglepoise lamp on the desk, gold glinted from his tie-pin, his arm-garters, the big rings on each of his hands and even the thin rims of the spectacles that he wore halfway down his pug nose. There was an unlit cigar stump in the corner of his mouth.

'Shut the door and come in, son,' he said. 'Pay no heed to the dogs.'

He pulled the cigar from his mouth and gave a husky chuckle. 'Aye, son, I've no need to lock the door when my wee girls are here.'

My eyes still darting down at the Alsatians, I closed the door and walked towards the man. I hadn't met the man before, but I knew him well from Dad's description. 'A wee, fat, tight-fisted bastard' was how Dad described P. Percy. He owned this shop in the Ferry and another two shops in Edinburgh; like all bookies, he was very rich. None of his customers knew what the 'P.' stood for, so they just referred to him as 'Percy'. His son, who was equally anonymous, was called simply 'Percy's son'.

Percy's son was the cherub I had seen at the hatch. He, too, sat on a swivel chair facing me. He was smoking a reeking, foul-smelling cigar, his elbow resting on a shelf under the hatch. There was a bulging cash drawer on the shelf, together with a rubber stamp and inkpad, a stapler, and a clumsy-looking adding machine with a big handle. The man was probably in his early thirties, a younger, but much scruffier, version of his father. His hair was uncombed, and there was a round bald patch on his crown, like a monk's tonsure. His shirtsleeves were rolled up, and a wide, flowery tie with an untidy knot lolled askew over his heavy paunch. His shirt was stretched so tight across the paunch that the lower buttons seemed hardly able to bear the strain for much longer. He wore crumpled, checked trousers, white socks and scuffed brown shoes. Seeing Percy's son close up like that, I still thought that he looked like a cherub; a very tarnished and shabby cherub.

Percy was speaking again.

'Tell me, son, how's your father?' he wanted to know.

I cleared my throat. I had been asked the same question a dozen or more times that day on my journey round the houses. I spoke quickly, the story perfected.

'He went into Bangour on Monday morning. They've been taking tests all week, but he thinks that they'll operate on him quite soon now.'

'That's good...' Percy was saying, but his son interrupted.

'Didn't I tell you, paw, that Derry should've been in the hospital months ago? The poor man was looking awfie bad.'

Percy nodded. 'Aye,' he murmured, looking down at the dogs. Then he said to me: 'Your Dad says that you're a good help to him; a good wee runner...'

'A bookie's runner's runner,' Percy's son interrupted again, grinning, pleased with his cleverness.

Percy scowled at him, but said nothing. He turned back to me. 'How old are you, son?' he asked.

I shifted uncomfortably. My flush was reappearing.

'Fifteen,' I muttered.

Percy re-lit his cigar and looked hard at me. His eyes were the same colour as the acrid grey smoke from the cigar.

'Well now,' he said. 'This wee job you're doing for your father, it's our secret, right? A secret between you and your father and us two here. Right? Otherwise, the Polis'll string us up by the balls.'

I nodded sheepishly.

'Okay, son,' Percy continued. 'What have you got for us today, then?'

I reached quickly into my jacket pockets. The heads of the Alsatians jerked up suddenly, then down again when the dogs recognised that no threat was intended. I placed the betting slips in Percy's left palm and the money in his right. Although I had tried to flatten them out before I left the house, the slips were still very crumpled. They were usually handed to me at the door, wrapped tightly around their stakes; clandestine, little packages for the bookie. The incongruous scraps of paper bore secret, coded messages of hope, and a bizarre array of nom de plumes that reflected the idiosyncrasies of their authors. When I opened them up and read them, it was like uncovering a conspiracy.

Percy hardly glanced at the slips before passing them to his son. The son swivelled round to face the shelf and began to pummel the slips with the circular rubber stamp. The stamp flew up and down in his hand in a flurry of thuds. Percy was counting the money, flattening out the notes and placing the change in neat little piles. Seven pounds, nine shillings and sixpence, I said to myself. I had checked it twice already and had tallied it with the lines. I had collected bets at about twenty houses. The smallest bet – my own – was one and six; the biggest was two pounds.

Percy finished counting and waited. His son was scrutinising the betting slips now, and alternately stabbing his forefinger into the adding machine and hauling at its big handle. The machine clacked and whirred each time. After a final tug of the handle, Percy's son tore off the piece of tally-roll and, with a loud bang, stapled it to the bundle of slips.

'Seven, nine and six,' he said quickly to his father and then turned his attention to the old man who had come to the hatch.

'Right, sir!' he shouted.

Percy smiled and nodded. He selected three half-crowns from one of the piles of change and handed them to me.

'A shilling in the pound,' he said. 'The same deal as your father.'

My eyes shone. It was a lot more than I had expected. A man's commission for a man's job. I took the coins from Percy's chubby hand and slid them quickly into my jacket pocket.

Percy sat with his fingers interlocked and resting on his belly. The cigar was dead again.

He said, 'That's a good wee round you've got there, son. We'll maybe get you collecting bets for the evening racing next week.'

I smiled for the first time.

Percy continued. 'Now, if you come back just before six, we'll have your returns for you. Right, son?'

'Right!' I said rather more loudly than I had intended.

I began to leave, but Percy was speaking again.

'We'll try and get in to see Derry some time next week.'

He looked at his son's back. 'Is that not right, lad?'

Percy's son didn't turn round. 'Aye, paw,' he said to the hatch.

The shop was busier and noisier now. The hollow voice crackling through the Tannoy speaker seemed to rise above the men's talk. My tread was more sure as I dodged past the men. My cheeks were still flushed, but there was a big grin on my face. Out in the fresh air, the sunshine dazzled me for a moment or two. My hand was still clutching the half-crowns in my pocket. I was seven and six richer; my bet might come up; and I was sure to get at least a couple of bob when I handed out the returns later on. I felt older, more mature. I wasn't just a spectator any more; I was part of the men's conspiracy, a co-plotter.

Walking back along the terrace, it occurred to me suddenly that they hadn't asked me my name. I thought of the two men – the father and the grimy cherub of a son – and their wealth and their corpulence. I thought of my own Dad in the hospital bed; the wiry, weather-beaten frame knotted in pain. Struggling on week after week while the ulcer seethed within him, spreading its poisonous tentacles, tightening its grip. Hiding the pain. Fear in those dark eyes. Compelled to carry on working. And I sensed it then about P. Percy & Son. Their concern wasn't real. Their sincerity was just about as strong and enduring as the tissue paper old Ma Reilly had used to write her line on that morning.

Later the following week, Mum and I visited Dad in the hospital. When we saw him, he was pulling hard on a roll-up, then tapping the dead ash into a little foil tray, the kind that come with apple tarts in them. The cigarette was not much thicker than the match he had used to light it; 'a Saughton special' he called it.

He chopped at the cloud of blue smoke with his left hand and said to us, 'The Sister doesn't like me smoking in the ward. She keeps threatening to take away my baccy tin. But I'm alright at visiting times.'

Mum sat at the edge of the bed with her back straight and her hands resting in her lap. She shook her head disapprovingly, but she was glad to see the twinkle in Dad's eyes. He looked rested, more relaxed. The pain and the worry and the tiredness that had creased his brow for such an interminable time seemed to have vanished. It was as if through his mere presence in the hospital he had found the key to unlock all of that unbearable pressure. Mum smiled and reached over to touch Dad's hand. They both knew that the hospital was only a temporary sanctuary. The worries were still lurking at home; the debt hadn't shifted. But he was in there to be mended; to return stronger and fitter and more able to take up the struggle again.

I sat opposite Mum, leaning back in my chair, listening quietly to the conversation between her and Dad. Dad spoke excitedly, almost boyishly, of the tests he had undergone. The barium meal sounded like a horrific ordeal. The hospital seemed to have completed its diagnosis, though: a huge pancreatic ulcer that stretched right across his stomach. Surgery to drain and then to remove the ulcer would be carried out later in the week. Mum pursed her lips and cursed the doctors in the Ferry for their incompetence; for their failure to take the problem seriously; for their insistence over many months that the ulcer could be treated with special diets and courses of tablets.

Deftly, Dad shifted her thoughts away from the bitterness. He began to describe the regime in the ward. The place appeared to be full of cantankerous, old men. Some of them were literally on their last legs, in there to die. A few had already passed away, silently, without struggle, in the middle of the night.

'I've figured it out,' Dad was saying. 'The old men that have been popping off have usually been in the beds right next to the ward doors. The closer they put you to those doors, the quicker you'll be offski, potted heid.'

I smiled and looked around the long ward, as if I was seeing it for the first time. There were about fifteen beds on either side of the ward, separated by a wide passageway. On a big, polished table in the middle of the passageway were two vases of flowers, several neat piles of books and magazines, and a box of dominoes with a splintered lid. Whispered, muffled conversations were being conducted at the few beds with visitors. Dad's bed was near the back of the ward, well away from the large swing-doors. Clearly, if his theory was correct, he was quite safe for the time being.

I looked past Mum and along the row of beds behind her. My gaze lingered on a bed that had seemed empty at first. The old man lay with his eyes closed, his white hair and grey face merged with the pillow, his skeleton of a body hardly furrowing the bedclothes. I thought that he was dead already. I dragged my eyes away from the spectre when I heard Dad ask, 'How are you getting on with that old skinflint at the bookies?'

'Fine, Dad,' I replied. 'He's paying me the full commission, you know. And I'm collecting for the night racing this week.' I paused. 'Percy says he'll be in to see you soon.'

Mum snorted. 'And pigs'll fly,' she muttered.

'That's good,' Dad said, as if he hadn't heard her. 'I've been placing a few bets myself. There's a wee man who comes in once a day. A runner for a bookie in Broxburn...'

'Jesus, Derry,' interrupted Mum, 'you're not still backing the horses. And in hospital, too. You can't keep away from the bloody things.' It had been twenty years since she had left Ireland, but the brogue was still as thick as the morning mists over the Liffey.

Dad grinned. 'It helps to pass the time, hen. Anyways, I'm a bob or two ahead the now.' He winked at me, and I knew right away that he had won much more than just a bob or two.

Mum checked her watch. We would have to go soon to catch the first of the two buses that would get us back to the Ferry. She stood up and said, 'I'll just away to powder my nose before the bus. Back in a minute.'

Dad and I watched her go, her back ramrod straight as usual, her heels clicking and clacking on the polished brown linoleum. She would be forty on her next birthday, a little heavier than before, a few traces of grey in the waves of blue-black hair.

Dad waited until the heavy doors had swung back into place. Then he reached out quickly, slid open the drawer at the top of the cabinet next to his bed and pulled out a piece of paper and a bundle of five-pound notes. He handed the paper to me.

'Right, son,' he said. The tone was hushed and urgent. 'I need you to do me a big favour. Have a dekko at that.'

I took the paper, a page of foolscap folded neatly in two, and I opened it up. The names of about forty horses were printed down the length of the page. A series of brackets to the left of the names grouped the horses into threes and fours. Further left was a complex set of betting instructions. Down in the right-hand corner of the page, a big circle highlighted the total amount of the stake, £50, and below that was the nom de plume, Aga Khan. I whistled and looked at Dad. It was the biggest bet that I had ever seen; a bet and a half.

Dad said, 'I'm trying out a new system. A new perm that I've read about in the form books. I've had plenty of time to work it out. I'm backing all the favourites and all the second favourites in every race from the three meetings on Thursday night. The way the perm works is that if only one or two of the horses are placed – which is a certainty – I'll get my stake back. But if they're all placed, I'll be rich. It's a good system, eh?'

I nodded, wondering if Dad was going mad.

He went on quickly. 'What I want you to do is to place the bet with Percy some time tomorrow. He knows my hand, though, so you'll need to write out the line again. But keep my one as a copy. Tell Percy it's from somebody that bides in the new houses up the back. I'd give the line to the wee man from Broxburn, but I'm not sure that he'd take it. It would be a big risk for him if it came up.'

He checked the swing-doors again and then thrust the notes into my hand.

'Not a word to your mother, mind,' he said. 'Just between you and me, I've made more money on the horses these past few days than from all the years of betting put together. And I'm intending to make a lot more with this new system.'

I just had time to stuff the paper and money into my pocket before the doors creaked open again. As Mum's heels click-clacked up to the bed, Dad asked me, 'Do you know who the Aga Khan is, son?'

I shook my head.

Dad smiled a wee, fly smile.

'He's the richest man in the world, son.'

On the Friday after that visit to the hospital, I was back at the end of the terrace with my chest pressed against the railings, staring down through the gap between the shops on the other side of the street, my thoughts lost for the moment in the patch of shimmering blue sea. The first week of the school holidays had brought glorious weather. Later on, once I was finished there, I would take a walk along the Shellbeds and see if I could find my pals.

The Jubilee clock struck the half-hour. I turned round again to face the padlocked door of the shop. Half-past twelve, and still they hadn't turned up. I had been waiting the best part of an hour already. I was growing anxious. Niggling thoughts were taking shape in my mind. It was as if a catastrophe had taken place, and I was the only person not to know about it.

With a sigh, I walked over to the shop, sat down on the stone doorstep and unrolled my copy of the 'Sporting Chronicle'. The sun was in my eyes, but I had little difficulty in making out the big red crosses that I had marked in the results section on the back page. Dad must have won a packet. More than twenty of his horses had been placed. Some of their odds were pretty high, as big as twelve to one for one winner. Now I was here waiting – and waiting – to collect the winnings...

I remembered the evening before when I had handed in the line, along with the handful of small bets I had collected round the houses. The front shop was deserted, and there was no sign of Percy or the dogs in the back office, just Percy's son, looking mean and surly and as dishevelled as ever. His hair looked like it needed a good wash, and his breath stank of stale beer. He was wearing a grubby pink shirt with a large polka-dot tie. He had stared cockeyed at the big, neatly printed line, eventually remarking, 'Aye, this is one of them newfangled perms. What fucking mug gave you this, son?'

I had shrugged and lied, 'Just a man up at the new houses.'

Percy's son had stared at the line for a moment longer, stamped it grudgingly and repeated 'fucking mug' under his breath. Then he had handed me a pound note, saying, 'A pound for cash, son. I can't give you any more than that. I'm taking too much of a risk already.'

That had bothered me a lot. But it didn't matter now; Dad

had managed to beat the bastards at long last...

A shadow fell over the newspaper. I looked up, squinting in the glare of the sun. The old man was tall and swaying a little. As if to challenge the warmth of the day, he wore a bonnet and a long black overcoat that was buttoned to the top. His hands were hidden in the coat pockets. His face looked white and frozen.

'Are you waiting for the bookies to open, son?' he asked in a loud, gravelly voice.

I nodded, still squinting up.

The old man stared blankly at the door for a few moments.

'Well, sir,' he said, 'you'll have a long wait, by Christ. In fact, you'll be waiting till the coos come hame.'

I abandoned my paper and stood up.

'What's wrong?' I asked.

The man took a big, gnarled hand out of his pocket and rubbed the stubble on his chin.

'I've just come from the Forth. Percy was on the phone to the landlord earlier. It appears that his big eejit of a son has fucked off to London with Percy's Jagyar and all yesterday's takings. He's done a bunk, son.'

I gaped. 'But I've got returns to collect...' I threw my hands up in despair.

The old man tutted.

'You're Derry's laddie, aren't you?'

I nodded.

'Well, if I was you, son, I'd go home and tell your father what's happened. Derry'll sort it out with Percy. It'll be alright as long as the lines haven't been burned. Okay, son?'

I nodded again and mumbled, 'Thanks, mister.'

The old man stepped down from the terrace and walked slowly in the direction of the next pub. I stood with my hands in my pockets, staring at the old man's back, dejection plain on my face. I turned quickly, fighting back the tears, and headed home. My hands were clenched into tight fists. I was angry and resentful... and afraid. Afraid of the pain that this would cause Dad. Afraid to see the hurt in his eyes again. I had seen it too many times. Like when the dockyard police strip-searched him and took away his lines. Or when Mum discovered where he had hidden the returns and then spent them all. Or when that drunken lout in the pub picked his pocket... It was the hurt that frightened the most.

We were back in the hospital the next day. The beginnings of tears were glistening in Mum's eyes.

'Jesus God, Derry, what have they done to you?' she murmured for perhaps the fifth or sixth time.

She was leaning over the bed, using a tissue to dab at the thread of saliva which seemed to be trickling perpetually from a corner of Dad's mouth.

'I'll be fine, hen,' he croaked. 'Don't worry yourself. It's just a wee bit of pain from the operation.'

He tried to sit up straight, wincing with the effort, inadvertently pushing back the covers to reveal the blood-flecked bandage around his stomach. There was a burn mark on the sheet beside him and a big brown blister along the index finger of his right hand. He looked at the hand and attempted a smile, but the smile appeared more like a grimace.

'Aye,' he muttered, 'they finally took my smokes away.'

Mum examined the blister and shook her head.

'Stupid eejit,' she said. 'Trying to smoke when you're still drugged to the eyeballs.'

I stood at the foot of the bed, holding on to the metal rail. The ward doors were on my left, only a short distance away. I was smiling across at Dad, trying desperately to mask the horror that I felt inside. His face was grey and haggard and lined with pain. His lips were drawn tight and pale. The pupils of his eyes were like tiny, dark slits. His pyjama jacket was open and looked much too large for his narrow shoulders and thin, bony chest. The sight of him reminded me of a picture I had seen in a book about the concentration camps.

Mum said something about seeing the Sister and then she moved quietly past me and out of the ward. I slipped into her place at the side of the bed. Dad peered at me for a moment or two, his eyes going in and out of focus. Finally, he wheezed, 'Are you looking after your mother, son?'

'Aye, Dad,' I answered softly. Tears were welling up in my eyes.

'You're a good laddie.' Dad grimaced again, trying hard to concentrate. It was as if he was struggling through a heavy haze. When he spoke again, the words were slurred.

'Did you put that line on with Percy okay?'

I gulped. My throat felt sore and constricted.

'Aye, I did, Dad,' I said. 'But when I went to collect the winnings yesterday, Percy's son had run off... to London. The bookies is closed down... and I'm not sure what to do next...'

Dad sighed, but there was no anger in his expression. His face seemed to soften a little, and I was sure that I detected the flicker of a smile. With a groan, he shifted up slightly and reached out to pat my hand.

'Never mind, son,' he said. 'It couldn't be helped. You'll not see Percy or the money again. I'll guarantee it.'

He sighed again and said, 'Who can you trust, eh?'

I looked at him, perplexed, wondering whether the reaction was coming from him or from the drugs they had given him to deaden the pain.

Dad raised his arm and winced. He pointed to the drawer of the cabinet next to me.

'Have a wee peek in there, son,' he wheezed and lay back again. 'Just a peek, mind. Then shut the drawer quick before your mother comes back.'

I opened the drawer an inch or two and glanced inside. My eyes opened wide and my mouth fell open. I jerked the drawer shut as if whatever lurked in there was on the verge of reaching out and grabbing me. On many occasions afterwards, I wished that I had taken a better look. Even now, I still can't believe that the drawer was stuffed full of money.

There was a proper smile on Dad's face now; the familiar smile of the quiet, fly, wee man from the Ferry.

'Aye,' he said, 'I kept a copy of the bet and managed to place it with the runner from Broxburn.'

He held up his left hand with two of the fingers crossed.

'See me and the Aga Khan, son? We're just like that...'

Mum came through the swing-doors, dabbing at her eyes with a handkerchief. She had just been told that there would have to be another operation to cut out the rest of the ulcer.

We were sitting in the kitchen on the day after the funeral, just the two of us, sipping tea, the solemnity of our expressions in perfect harmony with the greyness and dreichness of the early morning. The rest of the family were still in bed, still asleep, their minds and bodies recovering from the spent grief of the previous day and the rowdy get-together that came afterwards and went on through the night.

I sat opposite Mum, silently watching her. She looked cold and frail in her thin housecoat. Her hair had lost its lustre, and her eyes were puffy and red-rimmed. She was staring past me into nothing, her thoughts lingering on the edge of the abyss that was the future. She could sense only despair in that vast, unknown chasm: the despair of struggle and penury and aching loneliness. The bleak vista of widowhood was stretched out in front of her; a hostile and barren landscape.

My thoughts were also on the future. Unfairly, brutally, without warning, I had lost my father. There was bitterness in the loss and an immense desire to mete out blame, but I had to rise above those feelings and grasp the mantle of manhood that was being thrust at me. I was the man of the house now. I had to be my mother's comforter and supporter; her companion. I knew that there would be many times like this in the years ahead: silent, unspoken moments between the two of us.

Mum blinked and seemed to block out the abyss. She was back in the present, her mind on the immediate task of survival. Her voice sounded hollow in the quiet of the room.

'They all came yesterday,' she said. 'They brought their sympathy. And they drank their beer and whisky. And they talked and they sang about poor Derry. But not a one of them asked about the cost of the funeral. Not a one of them offered to help.'

She became silent again and looked down hopelessly into her teacup. Money, she thought. She cursed it. It had always been the bane of their existence. The cause of their unhappiness, their constant quarrelling. Surely the cause of Derry's death. Even the insurance policy had been surrendered long ago for the sake of the few coppers it had cost each week.

I was still watching Mum, staring into the misty softness of her eyes, searching for an answer. I was confused. She must have found out about the money in the drawer. She couldn't have forgotten so quickly, so easily. Why was she denying its existence?

I hesitated and cleared my throat. Finally, in a weak voice, I asked, 'Do you know that Dad had stacks of money in the hospital?'

She glared across at me, her eyes suddenly hard and cold.

'What money?' she barked.

It was as if my question had ignited the touchpaper of her emotions. I recognised it, but I also knew that it was too late to prevent the explosion. I had to persist.

Keeping my voice quiet, I said, 'Dad had a big win on the horses the week before he died.'

Mum banged her fist on the table. The teacups rattled in their saucers, shocked by her fury.

'Horses!' she cried. 'Bloody horses! A big win, my arse! Jesus Christ, he's got you as daft as he was!'

'But it's true, Mum. I saw it myself. Piles and piles of money in the drawer of the cabinet next to his bed. I saw it! Did you not collect it –'

'Collect it! Jesus Christ Almighty! I'll tell you what I collected from the hospital, will I? An ould watch. A ring. An empty wallet. And that stupid bloody box of cards with the names of his precious horses. That was it. That's what Derry left me. His life's worth. That's what I collected in a polythene bag.'

She wasn't shouting now, but the words were still spoken forcibly.

'So don't talk to me about horses. Or big wins. Or piles of money. Don't ever mention them again. Haven't I got enough on my plate already?'

Her anger used up, Mum buried her head in her hands and began to sob quietly. I reached out to hug her, to give her my warmth – and my forgiveness. Large, hot tears were rolling down my cheeks. I had stayed brave up until then. I hadn't cried at the graveside, nor afterwards, even when I had locked the door behind the last of the drunken relations. I was crying now. Tears devoid of bitterness. Tears of sorrow. The sorrow not for me, but for the man who had never won; the man who was destined to lose. They robbed him before he died, and they robbed him after he died. When I closed my eyes, I could picture that tired, gaunt face. And I could hear that sad, little sigh, and Dad saying, 'Who can you trust, eh?'

Chapter Thirteen

A Reward in Heaven

So that was the end of Dad's story. Which is just as well, because the bus is coming into Bathgate now. It'll be through Boghall and past the park in moments, and then that big, ugly school building will loom into view around the corner. I've only got seconds left to steel myself, to stiffen up, to make sure that I don't burst into tears at the slightest thing when I get off the bus.

    Like all those good and bad memories of Dad that I've just been through, my emotions are swirling about inside me. Mostly, though, I feel bitterness – and hate; hate for all those people who wronged him. I want to take vengeance on that spiteful, old man, McLucas; on that smirking thug, Pigeon Maudsley; on fat Percy and his greedy lout of a son; on that slimy thief in the hospital; on those big morons, Rob Lyle and Stan, the baker, for sniggering behind Dad's back and making the pain worse; on all of them. And not forgetting Mum; I love her dearly, but I can't help hating her for her complicity in Dad's destruction.

    The thing is that I don't want to keep on hating like this. Because that would destroy me, too. I don't want to keep remembering Dad as the grey, pained man that he was in his last months. I want a better memory than that. I want to remember him as the bookie's runner with the lopsided grin and the cheerful whistle. Here he comes along our street now. He's wearing his light grey suit and his striped tie. His fedora is pushed back on his head. He's dressed like Frank Sinatra, like a member of the Rat Pack. He's wheeling and dealing. He's thinking about his horses; about Arkle and Stalbridge Colonist and the others. And he's happy. That's the picture that I want to hold on to.

But there's another picture that lingers on in my mind. It's the morning of the funeral. I'm walking slowly behind the hearse, leading the procession from the Chapel up to the cemetery. We reach the top of Kirkliston Road, and suddenly they're there: hundreds upon hundreds of mourners, lining both sides of the road, cramming the little lane that leads up to the cemetery gates, filling the cemetery itself. It's as if the whole town has come to say goodbye to Dad. It's a measure of the love that people have for him – for their Derry McKay, for a son of the Ferry.

Some of those people told me that Dad was bound to get a reward in heaven, because he was denied one on earth. Well, I'm sorry, Dad, but what this journey through your life has taught me is that I'll be happy to forego the multitude at my graveside and my heavenly reward in order to live a better life than yours. I can never be like you, Dad. I won't ever be gentle and trusting. I've learned from your errors.

I feel stronger now that I've come to that conclusion. I'm more ready for today's battle and for the many battles beyond today.

About the Author

Brendan Gisby was born in Edinburgh, Scotland, halfway through the 20th century, and was brought up just along the road in South Queensferry (the Ferry) in the shadow of the world-famous Forth Bridge. He is the author of several novels and biographies and a mountain of short stories. He is also the founder of McStorytellers (http://mcstorytellers.weebly.com), a website which showcases the work of Scottish-connected short story writers.

Printed in Great Britain
by Amazon